A NEW ZION

THE STORY OF THE LATTER-DAY SAINTS

A NEW ZION

THE STORY OF THE LATTER-DAY SAINTS

BILL HARRIS

THUNDER BAY
P·R·E·S·S

San Diego, California

Thunder Bay Press
An imprint of the Advantage Publishers Group
5880 Oberlin Drive, San Diego, CA 92121-4794
www.thunderbaybooks.com

© Colin Gower Enterprises Ltd. 2004-02-18

All notations of errors or omissions should be addressed to
Thunder Bay Press, Editorial Department, at the above address.
All other correspondence (author inquiries, permissions)
concerning the contents of this book should be addressed to
Colin Gower Enterprises Ltd., Cordwainers, Caring Lane, Leeds,
Maidstone, Kent, U.K.

ISBN 1-59223-206-X

Library of Congress cataloging-in-Publication Data to come

1 2 3 4 5 08 07 06 05 04

DESIGNER: **Jack Clucas**

COLOR REPRODUCTION: **Berkeley Square**

Printed in Hong Kong

Contents

Foreword

by Wm. Budge Wallis

I am a product of the "New Zion." My grandparents responded to the gospel message carried by early Mormon missionaries in England, were baptized into the Church, and made their way across the Atlantic Ocean and the United States to the gathering place in the West. In time, I was born in a small Utah town where I was raised and taught the principles and practices of the Church, which I embraced.

I never tire of hearing about how the Mormon Church began, developed, struggled, and moved on to colonize the West. This book covers the story well, through the eyes of one who is not a member of the Mormon Church. He not only tells about the background and formation of the Church but brings the history up to our current day. The sacrifice and perseverance of the early Church members is impressive and inspiring in light of the hardships, persecution, and violence they suffered. But the real strength of the people was a spiritual strength flowing from restored principles, authority, and faith in God.

My grandfather, who joined the Church in England and became a successful publisher of newspapers in Idaho and Utah, stated time and time again that his most precious possession was his membership in the Church of Jesus Christ of Latter-day Saints. I am sure the other builders of the New Zion would agree.

Chapter 1

Revelations

The most powerful volcanic eruption in recorded history happened on the Indonesian island of Sumbawa when Mt. Tambora exploded on April 10, 1815. Few people in North America were aware of it, and almost no one was able to explain the persistent glorious pink sunrises and sunsets that the volcanic ash eventually created over New England and other places.

The following spring, a year after the disaster, flowers bloomed as usual and birds began flying south, but there was an ominous chill in the air. Farmers who should have been busy putting in their crops found themselves chopping ice instead. They all had faith that God would realize His mistake and right things again, but their hopes disappeared under a foot of snow that blanketed their fields in the middle of June. Temperatures rarely went above the forties after that until an early September killing frost set the stage for one of the coldest winters anyone could remember. New Englanders who lived through it referred to the year 1816 as "eighteen hundred and froze to death."

Even if large numbers of these people had drifted away from organized religions, all of them lived by the words of the Bible, and most of them were certain that the summer that never came and the brilliant colors in the sky were nothing less than signs and portents of Christ's imminent Second Coming. They believed that the time was at hand to get their spiritual lives in order.

The generation before them had been inspired by the first Great Awakening during the years leading up to the Revolutionary War. It began as a counterbalance to the Age of Enlightenment that was dawning in Europe at the time and seemed to be threatening age-old doctrines that had always been accepted on pure faith. The backlash began with revival meetings that were staged by the Presbyterians in the middle colonies, and the movement spread like a wildfire into New England in the hands of the Baptists and the former Puritans (who were calling themselves Congregationalists by then).

It was a rare sinner who wasn't touched by their message, which was that they should not follow their heads, but listen to the stirrings of their hearts instead. The thundering sermons that were the centerpieces of all of the revival meetings never varied. Human nature had become hopelessly corrupted, they thundered, and the unrepentant were all doomed to hell, the terrors of which the preachers weren't a bit shy about describing in gruesome detail.

The Great Awakening brought new members by the hundreds to the churches that sponsored revivals. But at the same time it widened an already existing social split among the Protestant denominations, the followers of each of which considered themselves superior to all of the others.

But the evangelists weren't able to reach into everyone's heart. Many chose not to be saved and remained unchurched. Others found their ardor cooled over time and began backsliding to their old ways. That is, until that strange summer woke them up again.

The second Great Awakening was, if anything, more intense than the first. There was a greater sense of urgency this time around. The traditional Protestant faith in the divinely inspired words of the Bible was augmented by a stronger emphasis on Jesus Christ as mankind's Savior, and the repentant were often gathered together for revival meetings at times and places that the preachers assured them was where His Second Coming was going to take place. When it didn't happen as predicted, they went home to their farms and villages to wait for the next call to witness Christ's return. It went on like that for months on end, and before long, disillusioned New Englanders, who were fed up with their rocky farms anyway, began drifting away to meet their Savior in a more congenial setting, hopefully a place where summer came around every year right on schedule.

Among the families that moved west from Vermont to the frontier of what they called "York State" was Joseph Smith Sr., his wife Lucy,

Below: *Main Street Palmyra in 1905, less than a hundred years after Joseph Smith's revelations. This was the nearest town to the Smiths' family farm.*

Joseph Smith the Prophet

Above: *Joseph Smith as a young man in the early 1820s.*

The third son of a hardworking farmer, Joseph Smith Senior and his wife Lucy, Joseph Smith was the catalyst that created this powerful new religion. Young Joseph was industrious, bright, curious about religion and he roamed the Mohawk Valley in his search for inspiration.

His attempts to find religious truth at organized revivalist meetings had failed, and his awakening now came in a series of divine visitations. These entrusted him with translating the sacred plates, to create an English-language version of the Book of Mormon. This was to be the cornerstone of the future church, which came to be known as the Church of Jesus Christ of Latter Day Saints.

Right: *the Smith Family's frame home in Manchester Township near Palmyra, New York State, which was recently restored to its original form.*

Opposite page, top: *A 1907 photograph showing a panoramic view of the Mohawk Valley with the Smith family Farmstead in the distance.*

Opposite page, bottom: *An early photograph of the road to Sacred Grove that Joseph Smith himself took.*

Below: *Sacred Grove today. The original site where Joseph received his revelations.*

and their eight children. They settled in a town called Palmyra along the Erie Canal southeast of Rochester where they lived in a rented house while everyone in the family who was old enough worked to accumulate enough money to make the down payment on a hundred-acre farm in nearby Manchester Township. After the money was accumulated, they cleared sixty acres of heavy wood for a wheat field on their new spread, tapped some fifteen-hundred sugar maple trees, and built a small log cabin. By the time they moved into their new home, their third son, Joseph Jr., had just celebrated his twelfth birthday and he was already joining his father and brothers as day laborers on local farms to help pay off the mortgage on their own.

Even before the Smiths moved into the Mohawk Valley, the population there had mushroomed, and circuit-riding evangelists were taking advantage of the opportunity to round up more converts. Their passion transformed the area into what was called a "burned-over district," a hotbed of religious extremism that no section of the country had seen before and hasn't seen since. A "holier than thou" attitude separated churches from one another, as it had in the previous Awakening, but this time it also led to the establishment of new beliefs, including the Seventh-Day Adventists, the Church of Christ, Scientist, and Jehovah's Witnesses. The Millennial Church, known as the Shakers, which had been imported from England during the first Great Awakening, came into its own as a major refuge during the second.

It was a confusing time for a lot of young people, including Joseph Smith. The revivalists focused their attention on the youth, who weren't yet set in their ways and were easily influenced by peer pressure, if not by the preaching itself, to "see the new light."

Young Joseph went to dozens of those revival meetings, but even though he was seriously concerned about the welfare of his soul, he just couldn't seem to get the spirit. Although he admitted that he longed to be able to "shout like the rest," something was holding him back. He was especially disillusioned by the competition among the ministers for converts. They seemed to be causing more bad feelings than good, he said. "I knew not who was right and who was wrong, but considered it of first importance to me that I should be right."

Joseph's search for answers led him to the New Testament and a passage in the Book of James. "If any of you lack wisdom," it read, "let him ask of God . . . and it shall be given him." Retiring to the wilderness, he began to pray fervently for the promised wisdom. At first he experienced an overwhelming power that took away his ability to speak. Then, suddenly, the grove was plunged into deep darkness,

Above: *Sacred Grove in 1905, a place that has a mystic quality.*

Below: *An artist's powerful re-creation of Joseph Smith's religious experience.*

even though it was the middle of the day. The boy felt that he had met his doom, but he continued to pray inwardly. As suddenly as the darkness had shrouded him, he found himself enveloped in a pillar of brilliant white light. Within the light were two human figures, one of whom pointed to the other and, after addressing Joseph by name, said, "This is my beloved Son. Hear him!"

After being told by the Son that his sins had been forgiven, Joseph recovered his powers of speech and asked which of the churches he ought to join. The answer was that all of their messages were false and that many of them were "corrupt; that they draw near to me with their lips, but their hearts are far from me." Joseph was sternly warned not to join any of the churches, but he was given an assurance that the fullness of a Gospel would soon be made known to him.

When the vision ended, the fourteen-year-old Joseph Smith found himself lying on his back looking up at the sky through the trees. For a time he was too weak to move, but he felt an indescribable peace and calmness. He said that, "for many days I could rejoice with great joy and the Lord was with me."

When he tried to share that joy, though, nobody would believe his report of the vision. The local Methodist minister echoed the general opinion by informing him that, "there are no such things as visions in these days; all such things ceased with the Apostles and there will never be any more of them."

But, of course, there would be more. Quite a few of them, in fact. Joseph Smith's first vision was followed three years later by a visitation from a white-robed figure who informed the boy that he was a messenger from God bringing word that the Father had work for Joseph to do. The divine messenger, who said that his name was Moroni, told Joseph that an ancient record of the early inhabitants of America was buried on a nearby hillside. It had been, he said, written by his father, Mormon, their last historian, and it was engraved on gold plates. The angel also told him that two stones called Urim and Thummim were buried along with the plates and could be fastened to a breastplate as a means of translating the book. That translation, he said, would reveal the fullness of the Gospel as it had been delivered by the risen Christ when He appeared to the ancients in North America.

Moroni told Joseph where he would find the plates and warned him not to show them to anyone once he had recovered them. The next day when Joseph went to the hill that he had been shown in the vision, the angel Moroni appeared to him once again. The angel said that Joseph's thoughts of potential wealth had turned him away from the original instructions, and therefore he was not yet ready to unearth the golden plates. Then Moroni commanded Joseph to revisit the hillside once a year for each of the next four years. Every time he did, Moroni was waiting there to give him more instructions and to reveal "what the Lord was going to do, and in what manner his kingdom was to be conducted in the last days." Joseph Smith was finally entrusted with the plates at the age of twenty-one, on September 22, 1827.

Joseph went right to work translating the history that the plates contained, but as he himself said, the engravings were in a form of Egyptian hieroglyphics that he, a barely educated young man, obviously couldn't decipher. But he had been given a decoding device, the pair of transparent stones, called Urim and Thummim, joined together by a bow resembling the rims of eyeglasses. Fastened to a breastplate, the person using them would be able to concentrate with his hands free. Joseph didn't reveal exactly how the process worked, but he reported that through them, he was able to translate the Book of Mormon "by the gift and power of God."

Although anti-Mormon literature sometimes ridicules the concept of a link to God through a pair of ordinary stones, it has a foundation in Scripture, whose origins are never questioned except by people regarded as blasphemers. Exodus tells us that God commanded Moses to craft a breastplate for his brother Aaron and to "put into this breastplate of judgment the Urim and the Thummim; and they shall be upon Aaron's heart when he goeth in before the Lord." The stones are mentioned several more times in the Old Testament as a sign of a direct priestly connection with God.

Although Joseph Smith never explained the translation process, it is generally believed that it didn't involve words magically appearing. Apparently he was forced to concentrate deeply to get an understanding of the meaning of the text, and step by step his conclusions were confirmed through divine intervention, after which he dictated the passages in his own words to a scribe, in most cases his wife, Emma, who worked behind a veil that hid them from the plates themselves.

The Book of Mormon, which resulted from this long labor, is an account of the original inhabitants of the Western Hemisphere who arrived in about 600 BC. It is divided into fifteen books, the first two of which, the First and Second Books of Nephi, describe how Lehi, a

Above: *The Angel Moroni, who appeared to Joseph to reveal the divine mysteries, is symbolized here as the statue that tops the Temple spire in Salt Lake City.*

Right: *An early drawing of the design for the Temple statue.*

Opposite page, top and bottom: *Two early pictures depicting Hill Cumorah, where Joseph Smith was directed to find the engraved records that came together as the Book of Mormon. The Church obviously set out to capture these images for posterity a century ago.*

descendant of Joseph, whose brothers had sold him into slavery in Egypt. Lehi, his wife, and their four sons and all their families had also been exiled into slavery, but eventually fled aboard a ship the Lord had commanded him to build. They were guided to a new promised land, which they called Bountiful, on the other side of the sea.

Two of Lehi's sons, Lemuel and Laman, rebelled, and their followers, who were called Lamanites, were cursed with dark skin and became the ancestors of the American Indians.

The next four books, Jacob, Enos, Jarom, and Omni, carry the narrative through more of the pre-Christian era in the Americas, and the three main books, Mosiah, Alma, and Helaman, recount the history of the Nephites, who were descended from Nephi, another of Lehi's sons. These books describe wars among the Lamanites and the creation of a formal Church, along with the establishment of the offices of High Priest and Chief Judge. They tell of the appearance of the Antichrist, Korihor, and the persecution of followers of the true Church.

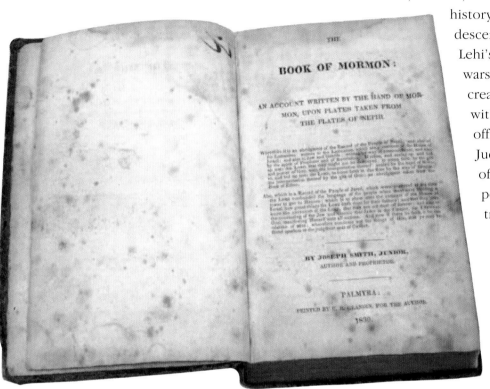

Above: *The original sacred Book of Mormon that shows Palmyra as its place of origin and the date 1830. Five thousand copies were printed at that time.*

These and other records continue in the Third and Fourth Books of Nephi, which tell of Christ's appearance to the people of Nephi whom He characterizes as the other scattered sheep of Israel that He spoke of in John 10:16: "And other sheep I have, which are not of this fold: them also I must bring, and they shall hear my voice." According to the narrative, Christ's teaching in North America after His Resurrection ushered in a period of general peace. The text also includes Christ's promise that Israel shall be gathered after the Book of Mormon came forth, and they would build the New Jerusalem.

The next book, called Mormon, describes the end of the peaceful times through sin and denial. It climaxes with a war between the Nephites and the Lamanites that resulted in the total destruction of the Nephites, although it is prophesied that the Nephite record shall one day come forth in a time of wickedness, degeneracy, and apostasy.

This last great battle took place on a hill called Cumorah, which was where, centuries later, Joseph Smith found the engraved records that came together as the Book of Mormon.

Although the Book of Mormon became central to the new Church, it is regarded as an extension of the Christian Bible and not its

replacement. While the Old Testament relates that the Jews were promised that they would gather in Jerusalem, the Mormons believe that the prophecy applied only to the descendants of Judah, one of the tribes of Israel, who ultimately refused to accept Christ. They regard themselves as the lineage of the more faithful tribes of Joseph and Benjamin, and they believed that it presented them with a mandate to establish a new Zion.

Although critics of the Church of Jesus Christ of Latter-day Saints often dismiss the Mormons as not being part of the larger Christian community—in spite of its name—the new era Joseph Smith was able to reveal was deeply embedded in Christianity with an emphasis on repentance and baptism and a restoration of the original Church of the Apostles. But it went a step further by restoring ancient Israel itself. While the early Christians had appropriated and altered the Judaic heritage, this new belief appropriated not only the Christian version of Judaism, but revived the Old Testament covenant as well. Mormons place great emphasis on the reliving of Old Testament events, and Joseph eventually restored the Hebraic priesthood and reestablished the Temple and its ordinances, making it a very real experience in the modern world. Very much like the first Christians, the Mormons began thinking of themselves as a fulfillment of ancient Hebrew prophecy, but although outsiders often see them as more Jewish than Christian, Jesus Christ and His kingdom is the centerpiece of Mormon belief.

The work of translation of the Book of Mormon was finished in 1829, and after it was copyrighted, Joseph's friend Martin Harris mortgaged his farm to pay for the printing of the first 5,000 copies. Harris, as well as Oliver Cowdery and David Whitmer, who had worked with him in transcribing the text, were given the privilege of looking at the original plates at that time, and their testimonies, along with those of eight other witnesses, are still printed in every copy.

But those few, along with members of the Smith family, were the only people with knowledge of this new revelation at the time. The Church still hadn't been organized. It didn't even have a name.

On April 6, 1830, a month after the Book's publication, thirty followers, including six who identified themselves as organizers of the new Church, gathered in a house in Fayetteville, New York, and, by a unanimous vote, named Oliver Cowdery and Joseph Smith as its first Elders. Among the concepts they established were baptism of adults by total immersion and the creation of a priesthood open to all male members through two orders, the lesser Aaronic and the greater, designated Melchizedek, who may bestow the gift of the Holy Ghost through the laying on of hands. The new structure called for Bishops to be appointed to administer their secular life, and a council of High Priests who would administer the sacred rites and rituals. In spite of their titles and responsibilities, members of the priesthood are still considered laymen and serve without pay.

Below: *A stylized early nineteenth-century illustration, depicting a rather dandified Joseph Smith with the Angel Moroni. Detailed in the picture are the stone tablets, the breastplate, and the spectacles that enabled Joseph to begin translation of the Book of Mormon.*

Above: *The April 6, 1830, gathering in Fayetteville, New York, where the structure of the new Church was formalized.*

The assembly's next order of business was to give the Church a name, and citing divine revelation through the Prophet Joseph, they agreed to call themselves the Church of Christ, a name they used over the next four years. During that time, another revelation led them to begin referring to themselves as "Saints," although outsiders, who they called "Gentiles," called them "Mormons" or "Mormonites," all too often sneeringly. To help shed what was becoming a negative image, the Church followed Joseph's revelation in 1834 and changed the name to the Church of the Latter-day Saints. Drawing from his revelations, which were contained in the Book of Mormon, the Doctrine of Covenants and The Pearl of Great Price, Joseph was inspired by the Lord's words "Thus shall 'my' Church be called in the last days, even The Church of Jesus Christ of Latter-day Saints."

By that time, the influence of these Saints had extended far beyond upstate New York, and they were making plans to establish a new city of Zion on the Missouri frontier more than a thousand miles away. But for them, the way of the Lord had been a hard one, and there were long, hard days ahead.

Chapter 2
Taking the Word to the West

Below: A romantic picture of Joseph Smith that captures his far-seeing sense of destiny as Church leader.

During the summer following the meeting in Fayetteville, the new Church attracted scores of new members. Though the growth was encouraging, the Saints were also attracting enemies at an even faster rate.

The old-time religion of the revivalists centered on the concept of being converted and coming to Christ, not to mention filling the collection plates of the established churches. The Mormons rejected this form of revivalism in favor of making a complete change in one's life, and they were making much stronger demands on potential followers. In their opinion, theirs was the one and only way to salvation, and reflecting the still-widespread belief that the Millennium was imminent, they warned that even devout churchgoers would have to join with them if they were to have any hope at all of being part of God's new kingdom on earth.

Naturally, the Mormon dogma made a lot of people uncomfortable. The preachers, who the teenaged Joseph Smith had noticed, had been feverishly building the size of their congregations and the extent of their own influence began turning their verbal cannons on the newly emerged Prophet. Members of their flocks who believed themselves to be already saved didn't much like having their beliefs challenged and their reaction was quite often violent.

Joseph Smith was arrested on trumped-up charges of disorderly conduct on two different occasions during that summer, and although he was acquitted both times, the Saints took it as a sign that they should turn the other cheek and take their religion to a more hospitable place.

Above: *A youthful Brigham Young, one of the Church's most illustrious early converts.*

Below: *The Church set out to convert American Indians, or Lamanites, who were recognized as the original people of North America. This policy was in sharp contrast to that of most other Christian religions of the time.*

Even if the Saints were foursquare against the kind of evangelism that had created the burned-over district of upstate New York, the Prophet Joseph had received a revelation that every male convert was to become a missionary, taking the Word to their friends, neighbors, and families. It was a similar idea to the practices of the born-again Christians, to be sure, but the difference was that each and every man in the Church was expected to spread the word—not just self-appointed preachers, as was the case among the other churches. The first missionary Joseph specifically appointed was his brother Samuel, who took copies of the Book into the countryside but came back with almost no converts. There was one notable exception, a young carpenter named Brigham Young.

Late in 1830, Elder Oliver Cowdery and three other missionaries were sent west to convert the American Indians, or Lamanites as they called them, but when they reached Ohio they found a more fertile field of potential Saints in a sect known as the Campbellites.

The religion had been founded by Thomas Campbell and his son Alexander, whose original idea was to reform the Presbyterian Church. But their work took a different turn when the younger Campbell met a powerful preacher named Sidney Rigdon, who convinced him that he would find bigger fields of converts if he joined the Baptist Church. It turned out to be a short-lived conversion, and Rigdon himself soon became a pillar of a Campbellite offshoot that he called the Disciples of Christ. After Cowdery and his fellow missionary Parley Pratt, himself a former Disciple, brought Rigdon over into the Mormon Church, more than 125 of his followers were baptized along with him. Then the missionaries moved on to nearby Kirtland, a crossroads village between the Lake Erie shore and Cincinnati. By the following spring, the Church had gathered more than a thousand members in Ohio's Western Reserve.

It was generally believed that Kirtland would be the site of the new Zion, and the idea was moved forward after Joseph received a revelation that he and his whole Church should move there from upstate New York. Indeed, as soon as he arrived, the Prophet ordered

The 19th Century Mormon Home

The restored interior of the Whitney Store, dating from the 1820s, showing the family living accommodation. This gives us a unique snapshot of domestic life in Mormon settlements such as Kirtland.

There are small touches of opulence, such as the long case clock. The movement may well have been brought from Europe and cased-in by local craftsmen. Possessions like these would convey some degree of status, but elsewhere, the room is fairly austere. The sanded floorboards are bare, and the wooden table and chairs are plain. The fire is a simple grate with a pair of cast iron firedogs, and the room would have been candlelit. The family's decorative possessions are stacked on shelves over the mantle. It is debatable how many delicate ornaments like these would have survived the rough trail west intact.

We know that Church organizational meetings were held in this room in the 1830s.

Above: *The N.K. Whitney Store in Kirtland, Ohio as it is today. See overleaf for a period photograph showing how accurately the store has been restored.*

Right: *The restored interior of the Whitney Store, dating from the 1820s, showing the family living accommodation. This gives us a unique snapshot of domestic life in Mormon settlements such as Kirtland.*

Below: *The interior of the store shows a stock of essential items. Besom brooms are recognizable, as are oven paddles, barrels of salt pork, dried meats, grain, flour, molasses, oil lamps, pitchers, pans, and some rather dainty chinaware. The iron stove would have enticed customers into the store on a cold day.*

construction to begin on a Temple and he presented a plan for a city of twelve Temples that would be able to serve a population of as many as twenty thousand Saints.

In the meantime, Joseph Smith and Sidney Rigdon had established a close relationship and together they established the Law of Consecration, also known as the United Order of Enoch, which was an attempt to put an end to land speculation at Kirtland by dedicating all property to the Church and returning it back to individual Saints who would develop and work the land. All surpluses were to be given over to the bishop, the head of the local church, to aid less-fortunate Saints. It was the first official promulgation of the concept of biblical tithing,

Right: *The store as it looked in 1907 when it was also the post office. Towns established by the first wave of Mormons often managed to survive, even after they had left. Their survival bears witness to the practicality of the hands that created them.*

which still requires the faithful to turn a percentage of their earnings back to the Church, either in the form of money or produce from their farms, or as donated labor. As it happened, Kirtland was already a well-established community, and the concept, which didn't apply to the Gentiles, didn't take a firm hold there. It caused hostility, in fact, and it was becoming obvious to the Saints that they would have to completely remove themselves from the world of the Gentiles if their own world was to survive and prosper.

Oliver Cowdery and Parley Pratt had moved on to the Missouri frontier and sent back word that it seemed to them to be the perfect place to establish the new Zion. The Prophet Joseph announced a revelation that it was surely so, and he and Sidney Rigdon, along with twenty-eight other Elders, moved across eight hundred miles of wild country to begin the work of building it.

Other Saints followed them. The land was quickly consecrated and a Temple site dedicated near Independence in what has since become a part of Kansas City. It was there in Jackson County that Joseph Smith was confirmed as President of the Church, and where he and Sidney Rigdon refined their United Order, incorporating many doctrines of the Disciples of Christ. The Saints thrived in the new land. Their membership grew to twelve hundred and their city was quickly becoming a showplace.

But their Missouri neighbors were less than impressed. They resented the Saints' pronouncements that God had given them this land.The Gentiles were worried that their own land was in danger of being given to the Saints too, although it was well-known that the Church had bought and paid for the land it occupied. They were also suspicious of the Saints' industriousness and of their uncommon thrift. To make matters worse, the Saints were friendly with the Indians, who everyone else in Missouri regarded as threatening enemies. And they seemed, to some at least, to be moving toward the abolition of slavery, an important factor in the local economy. Mobs routinely

Opposite page: *The magnificent Temple at Kirtland, Ohio, which was dedicated in 1836. Kirtland was a well-established community from which the Saints were wrongfully evicted.*

Below: *The sleepy rural outskirts of Kirtland in 1905.*

demonstrated, often violently, against the "Mormon scourge," and the final indignity took place in the Independence public square, where Bishop Edward Partridge and Charles Allen were captured by a mob and ordered to renounce the Book of Mormon and get out of the county. The Bishop responded by saying that if they abused him, they would be harming an innocent person. But he defiantly informed them that he was willing to suffer for the sake of Christ, as he didn't have the remotest intention of relocating.

The two men were stripped and covered with tar and feathers, but that wasn't the end of it. The mob came back a few days later and issued an ultimatum for the Saints to move on. When they appealed to the state's governor on grounds that their constitutional rights had been violated, he recommended hiring a lawyer. Meanwhile, the violence continued, culminating with what was remembered as the Battle of the Big Blue River. After two of the mob members were killed, the governor finally interceded and ordered the militia to disarm both sides. They did as they were told, but turned the Saints' weapons over to the mob, which left the Mormons without any means of defending themselves. That was when the Saints decided it would be better for everyone if they simply abandoned their homes in Jackson County.

Joseph was back in Ohio—where the Church's headquarters were at the time—while these things were happening, and he sent word that the attacks should be met with passive resistance. But as it happened, by the time his instructions reached his people, it was too late to even think about standing fast.

Those days were hard ones for Joseph Smith, as he found himself attacked by his own followers as a false prophet. A few of the people who had followed him from New York to Ohio, and some who had gone on to Missouri, were finding the way much harder to follow than they had anticipated. Some simply left the Church, but others stayed on to change the ground rules, which to them meant eliminating the Prophet Joseph.

But Joseph was able to weather the trials and he convinced the Kirtland Saints that they ought to be working even harder, beginning with a crash program to get their Temple built. When it was finished, the great stone building, which rose to a majestic height of 125 feet,

was the first real earthly home of the Latter-day Saints. It had cost as much as $80,000 to build, even though the actual labor was donated by the Church's male members.

A week after the dedication of the Temple in 1836, Joseph Smith and Oliver Cowdery said that Christ appeared to them there and said, "Behold, I have accepted this house, and my name shall be here, and I will manifest myself to my people in mercy in this house." They also claimed to have been visited by Moses, who bestowed the keys of the gathering of Israel on them; by Elias, who committed the dispensation of the gospel of Abraham; and by Elijah, who restored the keys of sealing to them. All of these were the working tools for the progress of the Lord's kingdom, and the manner in which they were delivered gave the Saints a whole new sense of purpose.

Joseph received many revelations during his years at Kirtland, but among the most far-reaching of them grew out of the grumbling of the disenchanted Saints. It moved him to declare that the future of the Church was going to depend on an infusion of new converts from abroad. Joseph approached Elder Heber C. Kimball and said, "Brother Heber, the Spirit of the Lord has whispered to me, 'Let my servant Heber go to England and proclaim my Gospel, and open the door of salvation to that nation.' "

While they were talking, Elder Orson Hyde, who had been one of the agitators, came into the room to announced his repentance and to volunteer for greater service. He got this wish and was set apart to join Heber on his mission to the British Isles. They baptized hundreds within a few short months, and Heber proudly recalled the Prophet's prediction that "God would make me mighty in that nation . . . [and] that I should be mightily blessed and prove a source of salvation to thousands."

A year after the Temple's dedication, the bank the Mormons had chartered failed in the nationwide panic of 1837, and the Church's leaders were left in debt to Gentile lenders to the tune of more than $150,000. It looked as though the end had come.

But the spark was still there. After the Missouri Saints were driven from Jackson County, they crossed the Missouri River into Clay County, where the locals were not only much less hostile but even appeared to be friendly and understanding. The Saints thrived there for three years before the old animosities came back to haunt them.

After they were not so politely asked to leave once again, they moved on to an unpopulated part of the state, where the Missouri legislature gave them the authority to establish their own county. They built the county seat at the edge of the prairie and called it Far West, which indeed it was. It was about as far west as any Americans had settled by then.

The Saints prospered in their own land, and the town attracted hundreds more of the Kirtland Saints. The ever-widening tide of

Below: *The restored Kirtland Schoolhouse. The original building was the cultural heart of the community, and it is typical of nineteenth-century schools all over America. The simple clapboard structure would have been furnished with wooden pews, a blackboard, and a single cast-iron stove.*

converts from England also arrived to swell their ranks even more. Before long the Kingdom of Saints was starting to run out of room and they began filling nearby counties, where the old problems with hostile Gentiles came back on them with a vengeance.

The Mormons had grown weary of turning the other cheek by then, and some of the militants among them formed an organization they called the "Sons of Dan" to defend the Church against the outsiders and to serve as defenders of the faith against wavering brethren inside the ranks of Mormonism itself. These bands, which followed the organization of the ancient Israelites in which groups dedicated themselves to defense, while others went about the business of building communities, were commonly called Danites. Over time, the Gentile community perceived them as a secret society of bloodthirsty killers, and they became the villains in a host of novels by the likes of Zane Grey and Robert Louis Stevenson. They were even exposed as murderers by Sherlock Holmes, although author Sir Arthur Conan Doyle's interpretation of them was as mythical as the detective he created.

Below: *The interior of the restored Kirtland sawmill. The foundations were discovered by accident, and the mill was re-created from early photographs of similar buildings that were constructed by Church craftsmen. Originally powered by water, the mill was capable of sawing logs up to sixteen feet long.*

Their influence was firmly established in 1838 by Sidney Rigdon who said in a Fourth of July speech that "we are weary of being smitten, and tired of being trampled upon . . . From this day and this hour, we will suffer it no more." He went on to call for all-out war against any mob that "comes on us to disturb us."

Those were fighting words and the fight began sooner than anyone expected it might. In that year's election, non-Mormons

gathered at polling places to deny the Saints the right to vote, by force if necessary. Force, as it turned out, was what was called for. Rioting broke out and the local authorities demanded that the Mormons should leave the county altogether. When they refused to move, a small but bloody civil war broke out.

The Saints went on the defensive and the town of Far West, as well as other nearby Mormon settlements, found itself under siege by the state militia that Missouri's governor had ordered to treat the Saints as enemies to be exterminated or driven from the state in the interest of "public peace." When Joseph Smith called for a truce, he and other leaders were jailed on charges of treason. Their trials were a mockery. One of the judges confided that he believed in their innocence, and that they should go free, but "[we] dare not administer the law, for fear of the mob." The Saints took this as a confirmation that the Gentiles felt they had a license to overrun them, robbing and physically attacking them as they did, and that there was no way that more mob violence could be avoided.

As far as the Mormons themselves were concerned, this was a sign from the Lord that the time had come for them to move on once again, rather than sacrificing more lives to a losing cause. But this time some eight thousand of them headed east into Illinois rather than pressing westward as they had done before. Joseph, who had been sentenced to be shot by a firing squad, managed to bribe his way out of prison along with the other leaders, and joined the exodus from Missouri. The war that drove the Saints out had cost them more than forty lives, not to mention their homes and all of their property. It prompted many Saints, including a few of the Quorum of Twelve, its ruling body, to abandon the Church altogether.

As had been the case with their previous setbacks, though, the Mormons regarded this as yet another manifestation of the persecution of the Saints of God for the sake of righteousness. It served to strengthen their conviction that they were, indeed, the people of God.

The Saints were more unified than ever by the time they crossed the Mississippi River into Illinois, and the well-publicized unfairness of their horrific experiences in Missouri had softened the hearts of Gentiles in all parts of the country. The message of this widespread sympathy seemed to be that the days of war and strife had finally come to an end.

In what appeared to be a confirmation of the new era to come, the local Illinois authorities welcomed the Mormons into their midst with open arms. These people, after all, were voters. More important than that, the state was still recovering from the financial panic that had nearly bankrupted the Church and the sudden influx of thousands of people well-known for their industry and thrift was like a gift from God Himself. That might very well have been the case.

But the Mormons weren't out of the woods yet.

Chapter 3
The Beautiful Place

Below: An early artist's impression of the Temple planned for the new settlement at Nauvoo, Illinois.

The Church had been blessed with well-organized leaders from the very beginning, and they systematically explored the surrounding area in search of a perfect spot, which they found about fifty miles to the north on a bluff overlooking a bend in the Mississippi River.

The Church's agents explored available land both in Illinois and Iowa to find a site for the new gathering of the Camp of Zion. They eventually settled on a 20,000-acre tract in Commerce, Illinois, that was available on a twenty-year lease at two dollars an acre. Other parcels nearby were also acquired on similar terms, and before long Joseph confirmed that it had been revealed to him that Commerce was destined to become the central gathering place of the Latter-day Saints, and he renamed it Nauvoo, which he said came from a Hebrew word meaning a "beautiful place of rest." The State of Illinois granted it a charter almost immediately, and the federal government added its own blessing by giving the new name to its post office.

The new entity, which was to become the headquarters of the Church, was established as a virtually independent city-state. Its city council was granted the unprecedented authority to "make, ordain, establish and execute all such ordinances . . . as they may deem necessary." No other city in America had been granted as much independence as this. For the first time, the Saints had been given the right to self-determination within the United States, and at the same time they were assured of being able to live apart from it.

Many of the Saints settled in nearby towns or established farms, but Nauvoo was the natural center of it all. After just four years of building it from scratch, a visitor described the place in 1843 as a beautiful city with "handsome stores, large mansions and fine cottages." He also remarked on the Nauvooites themselves as a "wonderfully enterprising people." As one testimony to their enterprise, the wood for houses and stores had not been cut locally, but rather in far-off Wisconsin by Mormon lumbermen sent north to find the best.

Their primary mission had been to find materials for the building of the Temple, whose cornerstone was laid on April 6, 1841, the eleventh anniversary of the Church's founding. The planned white limestone building was to be sixty feet high, with a tower and steeple rising up more than 200 feet. Even as it was being built, the Prophet preached to his flock at outdoor gatherings on the construction site. Over the months he established several new doctrines that were still being revealed to him. Many of them, which have been faithfully recorded in the Pearl of Great Price, were organized into the new Temple ordinances, among them baptism of the dead to reach out to those who had died without the benefit of receiving the Mormon gospel, and the endowment ceremonies, which confirm the living Saints' close relationship with God. These secret rituals can only be performed in a consecrated Temple.

There are more than one hundred Temples around the world today, and the number is growing, but regular worship takes place in chapels or meetinghouses. In order to be admitted to the sacred confines of one of the Temples, a Church member must have a valid "Temple recommend," which is given after a deep interview with the local Bishop and with the stake President. The questions involve such things as regular church attendance and the paying of tithes, as well as loyalty to Church leaders and close adherence to the Word of Wisdom, which prohibits the use of coffee, tea, alcohol, and tobacco. The recommend permits the bearer to take part in Temple rituals, such as baptism of the dead, for a period of two years—as long as he or she remains worthy. Only about 20 percent of all Mormons have this privilege.

Celestial marriage and the sealing of children to parents are important Temple ceremonies, and they are performed for both the living and the dead, transforming mortal bonds into eternal ones. Baptisms performed within the Temple are only for the dead. The living are baptized in the meetinghouses.

There was a dark cloud on the horizon as the Saints established their earthly kingdom at Nauvoo. Although the Mormons consistently denied it, Joseph had been given a revelation in the early 1830s confirming what he characterized as the "Patriarchal Order of Marriage." What everyone else called "polygamy" was quietly introduced among the Church's highest leaders, justified by Joseph and others as a continuation of the tradition of the Hebrew patriarchs, all of whom had multiple wives.

Below: *A fine painting of the Nauvoo Temple, which was in use by 1845. Ultimately, the decision to abandon this settlement meant that its construction was largely in vain.*

In letters and private journals, the Prophet said that he had been given a revelation that Temple marriages stood for all time, and family units would continue through eternity. Those whose marriages weren't sealed in the new covenant, he explained, would become ministering angels in heaven, but they were doomed to serve without exaltation. On the other hand, those families baptized and sealed in the Temple as believers in the Mormon gospel were promised the inheritance of "thrones, kingdoms, principalities . . . [And] they shall be gods because they have no end." In a society made up of more women than men, he implied that it was a man's duty to marry more than one woman as a means of guaranteeing their godly existence in the afterlife.

Another of Joseph's revelations was that there were unborn souls in heaven waiting to begin their journey on the path to godliness through an earthly existence, and that it was incumbent on the Saints to give them life on earth. The concept of plural wives made bringing these souls forth into the true religion more likely, he said.

Although most of the early Mormons were as repulsed by the idea as the Gentiles who cited polygamy as evidence that the Latter-day Saints were secret sinners, the practice went on even if Joseph Smith was very careful not to make it a part of the Church's official doctrine.

Not long after he arrived at Nauvoo, the Prophet permitted publication of a pamphlet defending plural marriage, although he was quick to disavow it in the face of a strong negative reaction from his followers. But the world outside was about to receive titillating evidence that the denied practice was indeed quite real.

A convert named John C. Bennett had made a name for himself as a major general in the Mormon militia, the Nauvoo Legion, and he had become the city's first mayor, as well as a close associate of the Prophet himself. He was delighted to be given the privilege of participating in the Patriarchal Orders, and he didn't waste any time seducing scores of young women. Joseph strongly objected that he hadn't bothered to seal his relationships in the Temple rites and that these women were his concubines and not his wives. After angrily confronting Bennett, Joseph ordered his excommunication.

The former mayor left town after that and took up a new career as a crusading journalist. His exposés of the lives and customs of the Nauvoo Saints appeared in newspapers across the country and readers couldn't get enough of them. He went into great detail about Joseph Smith's private army, the Nauvoo Legion, which he himself had led. And he offered insight into the workings of the Danites, whom he characterized as little more than murderers for hire.

But what caused the greatest stir were his lurid descriptions of what he saw as licentiousness within the Church leadership, although he neglected to mention his own leanings in that direction. He "revealed" that the Prophet Joseph, along with all of the Church's leaders, had several wives, including some, he said, who were also married to other men. He charged that his own excommunication had been the result of a rivalry between Joseph and himself in the pursuit of Sydney Rigdon's beautiful daughter, Nancy. Bennett's insider revelations served to fan the smoldering fires of Gentile hostility, and they caused a backlash within the Mormon community as well.

Most of what Bennett wrote was either untrue or grossly exaggerated, but the inescapable truth was that polygamy was, in fact, practiced among the Mormon leaders. Although more often than not its existence was denied, Brigham Young, who had twenty-seven wives of his own at the time, publicly revealed the doctrine of celestial marriage in 1852, and in spite of the denials over the years, polygamy was finally officially denounced by the Church forty years later.

While Americans were expressing indignation over Bennett's exposés, Joseph Smith himself stayed above the battle. He turned instead to the world of politics. The Saints had more or less voted as a bloc for Whig candidates over the years, but in 1842, the Prophet suggested that they ought to switch their allegiance to the Democrats.

Of course, the Whigs weren't too happy about that, and as it turned out the Democrats weren't exactly pleased either. Joseph's attitude suggested that he was creating a political steamroller that had the potential of putting his Church at the head of the government. Even though they had generally come to tolerate the Mormons, the Gentile community had no stomach for giving them that kind of power.

Unsuccessful in influencing the leaders of either party in his efforts to get public funding for the Church's loss of property in Missouri, Joseph announced his own third-party candidacy for the presidency of the United States. He was confident that the extensive Mormon missionary network, which now extended into every corner of the country, could gather votes for him. They themselves enthusiastically agreed.

Joseph was on the campaign trail in 1844 when William Law and Robert D. Foster, representing apostates who had fallen away from the Church, published the first issue of a newspaper they called the *Nauvoo Expositor*. From within the heart of the Mormon camp, the paper roundly attacked the Saints for their polygamous ways, for their grasping at political power, and for what the editors charged was pervasive financial recklessness. Joseph met them head on. He sent a message demanding that a special session of the Nauvoo City Council issue an official statement that the *Expositor* was a public nuisance and a threat to the peace. He also called for an order to smash its presses.

If the American public had been willing to look the other way on the polygamy issue, this blatant attack on freedom of the press was completely unforgivable. Conveniently ignoring the fact that Mormon newspapers had been silenced in the same way back in Missouri, angry mobs began surrounding Nauvoo within days. They petitioned Illinois governor Thomas Ford to call out the militia to join them, and when he refused, the militia mustered on its own and pressed the attack. The exasperated governor responded by asking the Mormon leaders to surrender themselves to him with his personal guarantee of protection and a fair trial.

Below: *An early illustration of the two Smith brothers, Hyrum and Joseph. Both are shown carrying fashionable walking canes. Examples of canes owned by Joseph Smith have survived to this day.*

Above: *A stylized lithograph of the assassination of the Smith brothers.*

The night before they were to give themselves up, Joseph, his brother Hyrum, and two of the Elders crossed the Mississippi intending to flee to the Rocky Mountains, but the Prophet's wife, Emma, sent word that they should come back, pointing out that they were leaving the city leaderless and without anyone for the Saints to turn to when they needed advice. Joseph took her advice, and the following day the four fugitives made their way to Carthage, the county seat, and turned themselves in.

They were formally charged with inciting a riot, destroying private property, and conspiring to establish an independent kingdom within the borders of the United States. The two latter charges weren't mentioned in the initial hearing and bail was set on the first at $500. But when Joseph, Hyrum, and the others left the courthouse they were arrested again—this time on a brand-new charge of treason—and jailed without a hearing.

They weren't locked up in a cell, but rather confined to a second-floor furnished room, where they were allowed to receive visitors. The following day, Governor Ford reduced the guard around the jail and then set out for a peace conference at Nauvoo after reassuring Joseph that he was still in safe hands. "You are unnecessarily alarmed for your friends, sir," he said, "for the people are not that cruel."

But the governor was quite mistaken. Not long afterward, John Taylor, one of Joseph's fellow prisoners, looked out of the window and saw a group of armed men, their faces blackened, slithering

across the field in the direction of the jailhouse. The prisoners heard loud laughing and joking among their guards downstairs, and then they heard the ominous sound of the jail door being smashed in.

The intruders rushed up the stairs toward the second-floor room and broke the lock on its door with a pistol shot. Then a second shot hit Hyrum in the face. It was followed almost immediately by another bullet fired through the window that hit him in the back, killing him instantly.

Joseph had a pistol in his belt, and he fired three shots into the mob through the closed door. But it wasn't enough to stop them. When the intruders began forcing the door open, John Taylor turned and ran to the window, where he was struck down by a bullet that hit him in the thigh. A second bullet aimed at his chest was stopped by his pocket watch, and he was spared to serve the Church in other days.

Joseph headed for the window too, but before he could jump, bullets struck him from both inside and outside the building. His body crumpled on the windowsill and then toppled lifeless over onto the footpath below.

Elder Willard Richards, the fourth Mormon prisoner, wasn't hurt in the incident, and the governor persuaded him to write an open letter to the Nauvoo Saints pledging that there wouldn't be any reprisals. He needn't have bothered. When the bodies of the martyrs were returned home, the entire population turned out, and although they were angry in their grief, there wasn't even a hint of violence.

More than twenty thousand of the faithful filed past the bodies as they lay in the unfinished Temple, and later nearly as many gathered on a nearby hillside to silently watch the coffins being lowered into the earth. But only a few of them knew that the pine boxes were filled with sand. The bodies themselves had been secretly buried in the cellar of an unfinished house where Church leaders believed they would be safe from more attacks by the outsiders.

The outsiders were convinced that without their Prophet, the Latter-day Saints would soon disintegrate and disappear from their midst. But they didn't understand the Saints or their Prophet. Joseph's martyrdom had provided his followers with the final, incontrovertible connection between themselves and Christ's original Church: the death of its leader at the hands of a mob.

There was no anticipated resurrection, of course, but the Latter-day Saints had the next best thing, a charismatic leader named Brigham Young who had been in their midst every step of the way in their fifteen-year search for the promised land of Zion.

Left: *The fine monument to the Smith brothers on the grounds of the Carthage Jailhouse in Illinois, a stone's throw away from the spot where they fell on June 27, 1844.*

The Smith Martyrdom

On June 27, 1844, while imprisoned in Carthage Jail in Illinois, Joseph Smith and his brother Hyrum were killed by a mob that stormed the jailhouse. Charged with inciting a riot, and, worse still, conspiring to set up an independent kingdom within the United States, the Smith brothers and two prominent Church Elders (John Taylor and Willard Richards) were incarcerated.

The incensed mob rushed the building, broke down the doors, and fired into the room, killing Hyrum outright. Joseph himself succumbed to a hail of bullets as he tried to escape through the window. John Taylor and Willard Richards were spared, and Taylor later became the leader of the Church.

Outsiders were convinced that this would be the end of the Church of the Latter-day Saints, but the massacre actually paved the way for a charismatic Brigham Young to lead the Saints on to freedom and New Zion itself.

Above and right: *Carthage Jailhouse. The scene inside the upper floor room where the four prisoners were held.*
Right inset: *The dramatic scene outside Carthage Jail, where Joseph Smith's body is lying. A ray of light from heaven beams on his attackers to demonstrate their guilt.*

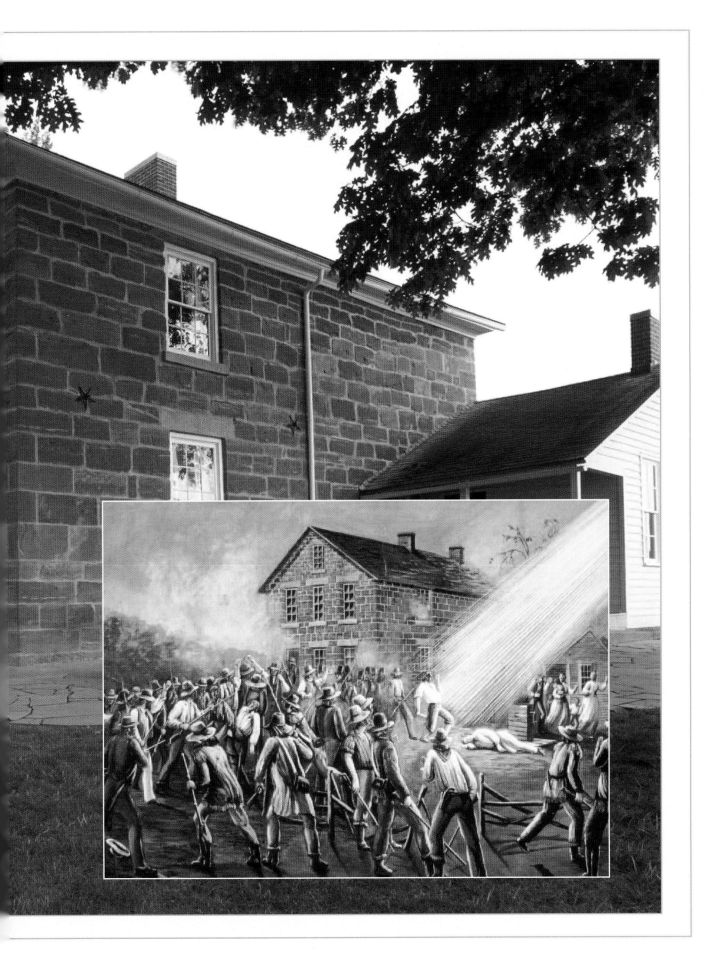

Chapter 4
Gathering Zion

It wasn't a foregone conclusion that Brigham Young would succeed the Prophet. Hyrum Smith, Joseph's brother and the appointed patriarch, had been the most likely candidate, but he was dead. And the Prophet's own apparent choice, his eldest son, also named Joseph, was only twelve years old, which put him out of consideration, too. Among the other most likely successors was Sidney Rigdon, who had served longest as the Church's first president.

The ultimate choice of a leader was in the hands of the Quorum of Twelve Apostles, whose members were scattered for the work of Joseph's abortive election campaign. The first to arrive back in Nauvoo for deliberations was Rigdon, with what he claimed was a revelation from the Lord that he had been chosen as a "guardian" to lead the Saints from their tribulation. His two-hour speech to the membership was impressive, if not a bit heavy with an attitude of doom and gloom about the Church's future, but it wasn't nearly as electrifying as the oratory of Brigham Young, who followed him.

Below: *Brigham Young, painted with a statue of a lion, is depicted outside one of his Salt Lake City residences. The allegory is obvious, as he proved to be a fearless leader of the developing Mormon community.*

Above: *A photograph of the completed Temple at Nauvoo. Just like the Temple at Kirtland, this Temple was also abandoned. The original Temple was destroyed by fire in 1848.*

In Mormon legend, it has been said that Brigham spoke with Joseph's voice that day, and many swore later that he looked for all the world like a reincarnation of the Prophet himself.

Brigham was unanimously elected as the Quorum's President, and his first act was to proclaim that the institutional structure Joseph had built should be carried on without any changes, although he tightened a good deal of it in the interest of efficiency, a Mormon hallmark. Apart from his worshipful regard for the work ethic, Brigham Young was almost fanatical about efficiency.

He also strongly believed that hard work was the Church's salvation and his first orders were that work on the Nauvoo Temple should be stepped up right away. He also called for an even more intense missionary effort, both back in the East and in Europe. He himself had served as a missionary in England, and he knew better than anyone how important the effort was going to be to the future of the Church.

There were several others who, like Sidney Rigdon, claimed that they had received divine revelations that it was they, and not Brigham, whom the Lord had chosen to carry on Joseph's work. Among them was James Strang, who even backed up his claim with metal plates that he said were missing parts of the Book of Mormon. He went on to lead one of several schismatic branches of the Church, the Reorganized Latter-day Saints Church, which he founded in 1860, and which still exists today with about a thousand followers.

Other leaders who disagreed with Brigham's authority took matters into their own hands and led small groups away from Nauvoo to establish Mormon outposts in the West. The Twelve met this trend head-on by directing their energies to finish building the central gathering place. The sounds of hammers and saws filled the air, and impressive new houses, many of them of brick, began to turn Nauvoo into the showplace it had always promised to become. It grew into the biggest city in the state, bigger even than Chicago, in fact, at a time when the Gentiles were convinced that the Mormon Church was on the ropes.

Top priority was given to finishing the Temple so that sacred endowment ceremonies could be held. The work had progressed far enough by December 1845 for the first of the rites to be conducted, and in less than three months, more than 5,600 Saints were endowed as God's people. Ultimately, about 6,000 Saints received their endowments in ceremonies that took place around the clock. There was an air of

Above: *The Mormon Tabernacle Choir performs at a weekly service at the newly reconstructed Nauvoo Temple.*

Left and below: *Architectural details of the Temple at Nauvoo. President Gordon B. Hinckley ordered the Temple to be reconstructed as a memorial to those who survived the flight from the settlement.*

urgency connected with these ceremonies, which can only be conferred within the confines of a Temple, because Brigham and his closest advisors knew that they would soon be far away from one.

The Church's leadership had been planning a new exodus for some time, and they knew it would make the Nauvoo Temple a place without a future. But they kept silent about their plan, even as the harassment from outside intensified through the summer and early fall, with outlying Mormon settlements being burned to the ground and farmers murdered in their fields. Brigham's response to the new atrocities was to order an evacuation of the rural settlements. He told the people affected that they must sell their property and remove themselves to Nauvoo, but he never hinted to any of them that Nauvoo itself was about to be abandoned.

Brigham finally broke his silence in October of that year, revealing that the Quorum had made plans to evacuate about 6,000 people in the spring, with more to follow as soon as they could be outfitted for a journey to the west. The Saints worked into the winter, organizing themselves into emigrant companies and building wagons to carry their belongings. By the end of November, 1,500 of them were ready to roll, and some 2,000 more were nearly finished as well. The Council of Fifty, which had been organized to oversee the exodus, designated an advance company of about a thousand men and scheduled them to leave in the spring to scout appropriate routes across the prairie and to establish campsites at intervals along the way.

But no one was quite sure exactly where they were going. During their time in Missouri, Church leaders had learned a great deal about the country to the west through dealings with Indians, explorers, trappers, and mountain men, and they were well aware of the advantages and potential pitfalls of just about every part of it.

The Oregon Territory seemed to be the most likely destination, but Brigham personally favored the Great Salt Lake Basin, which had been shown to him in a vision. So many pioneers were heading to the Pacific Northwest that they were in danger of being surrounded by Gentiles out there—which was exactly what they were relocating to avoid. But the Great Basin seemed to be out of the question, too, because it was still Mexican territory and the federal government was opposed to allowing its citizens to settle there. California also loomed large in their speculation and, in fact, 238 Saints from New York City, led by the flamboyant and impetuous Sam Brannan, began the long ocean voyage to San Francisco on February 4, 1846. It was the very same day that the first contingent of Saints left Nauvoo for the overland trip into the unknown, but in their case, the departure was quite sudden and not at all according to the plan.

That plan had been to start the exodus in April when grass on the prairie would be high enough to feed their livestock and ice in the streams would have melted. In anticipation, the Nauvoo Saints had

A New Zion: The Story of the Latter-day Saints

Previous pages: *The final battle for Nauvoo. The town was besieged by militia and defended by the remnants of the Nauvoo Legion. Constant persecution of this kind made the decision to move westward inescapable.*

Above: *An early photograph shows an orderly, but deserted Nauvoo, after the departure of the Saints on their trek westward.*

Opposite page, right: *A romantic composition shows the Saints crossing the Mississippi in around 1846. It was the first stage of their journey west. In the background, the Nauvoo Temple is already on fire, though in reality it wasn't destroyed until 1848.*

gone about the business of selling their property and using the money to outfit themselves for the journey ahead. But then everything changed. The Gentiles were at it again.

The first attack came in the courts as Brigham and several Apostles were charged with allowing counterfeiters to operate within the Nauvoo city limits. In the heat of the debate, the state revoked the city's charter, even though the charges were dropped. That storm had no sooner passed when Governor Ford sent unproved reports that federal troops were on the way to put a stop to the planned evacuation.

The Quorum of Twelve decided that, rather than wait for proof of the governor's warning, the exodus must begin immediately. About two thousand were ready to go by then, and thousands more said that they were close to being able to follow. The first of them crossed the Mississippi in small boats and barges, but about two weeks later, the river froze hard enough for the emigrants to cross with their wagons and supplies, which speeded the evacuation considerably. After the thaw, they used flatboats to deal with the first hurdle, as they had originally planned, and by the middle of May, it was estimated that some twelve thousand Saints had reached the west side of the river. There were about six hundred left behind in Nauvoo, most of them too poor, too old, or too ill to attempt the journey.

As the movement out of Nauvoo went on, work continued on the Temple. It was formally dedicated in April and abandoned on the same day. A committee had been formed to find a buyer for the building, but they came up empty. The building was simply delivered over to the Lord. On the brighter side, an estimated 90 percent of the Saints reported that they had been able to sell their own property, although usually at deflated prices and often in exchange for worthless paper.

The fact that there were a few hundred Saints still in the city prompted the Gentiles to assume that the promised exodus was a fraud. That was a convenient excuse for the militia to attack with rifles and cannons, but the remnants of the Nauvoo Legion set up blockades against them. The resulting siege lasted for three days before a truce was finally called. Under its terms, the remaining Saints surrendered their city in exchange for safe passage across the river. The mob retreated, but not before torching the new Temple. It was completely destroyed by the fire except for the front wall, which was eventually taken down by a tornado, seen by many as the work of the Lord. The last Saints to cross didn't go any further than the west bank of the river, where they formed what they called the "poor camp" and settled down in full view of the abandoned dream city that they had helped to build.

A young man whose curiosity led him to Nauvoo soon afterward reported finding mostly brand-new houses, nearly all of which were surrounded by well-tended gardens. "It was a pleasant morning," he wrote, "but not a woman could be seen in any of the green gardens." The great city of Nauvoo had been reduced to a ghost town.

Chapter 5
The Way of The Lord

The first group of Saints who crossed the Mississippi River in February 1846 didn't waste any time moving on across the hard-frozen, snow-covered prairie. They made their first camp among the trees lining Sugar Creek, which they renamed Brook Kedron, about nine miles into Iowa.

Those who had wagons used them as windbreaks, some pitched tents, and others built huts of quilts and strips of bark to keep out the bitter cold. The men cut trees and built huge fires where the refugees gathered to sing hymns, pray, and listen to the comforting words of the Church Elders. No one is certain how many people were in the camp, but on that first night, nine more were added, babies born to women who only the night before had been warm and comfortable in solid homes back in Nauvoo. Many more babies would be born homeless along the trail ahead.

More Saints arrived the next day, and still more during the days and weeks that followed. Among them was Captain Pitts's Brass Band, whose members

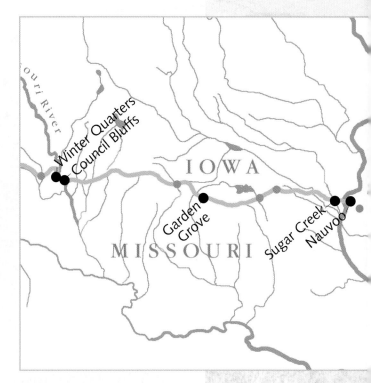

Above: *The trek across Iowa from the Mississippi River to the Missouri River.*

Above: *A covered wagon of the type used on the journey west. This was luxurious compared to the handcarts that were used later.*

had converted as a group back in England, although to the shivering emigrants, their music was a constant reminder of better days, both in the past and in times to come.

One of the band members, William Clayton, who also served as Brigham's scribe, gave them a special kind of hope with a hymn he called "Come, Come Ye Saints." Its final stanza reminds them:

> 'Tis better far for us to strive
> Our useless cares from us to drive;
> Do this and joy your hearts will swell.
> All is well! All is well!

By the time Brigham himself arrived at Sugar Creek on about the tenth day, he found his people doing about as well as he could have hoped. The shelters had been made more winter-proof by then, and a blacksmith shop had been set up to get the wagons ready for what lay ahead. The Temple guard had reorganized itself and had even built a parade ground in the center of the camp. Brigham was also pleased to hear that many of the men had gone out to work for local farmers, doing such things as building fences and cutting firewood in exchange for much-needed grain, a practice that would continue as long as their route took them near enough to farms and settlements.

Above: *The Saints crossing the frozen Mississippi.*

But Sugar Creek wasn't any great gift from a munificent God by anybody's standards. With more and more people, food was in short supply, the trees lining the creek had nearly all been cut, and the fires grew smaller in spite of the below-zero temperatures and the blowing snow, whose weight caused tents and lean-tos to collapse. Just about everyone was suffering from painful frostbite, and the contagious Mormon cheer was starting to fray into sullenness. It was clearly time to move on, and Brigham was quick to issue the order.

Following the plan that had been worked out back in Nauvoo, the Camp of Israel was organized, in military fashion, into tens, fifties, and hundreds, with officers appointed to look after each unit. The first contingent started west on March 1, headed, as one of the Elders put it, "we know not where."

Brigham Young himself, on the other hand, had already made up his mind by then. Following the lead of his earlier vision, the new Zion was going to be in the Great Basin. But what he and the Apostles didn't know for sure was exactly where the actual site might be—the Basin covers nearly 4,000 square miles. They also had no idea when they could expect to arrive.

If their first day on the trail was to be any indication, that arrival date was a long, long way off. The detachment of about 3,000 people and 500 wagons only managed to travel about five miles that day, and

Above: *A naive view of life on a wagon train.*

Left: *A cheerful depiction of the Saints passing through Iowa, pushing handcarts. The reality was far harsher.*

many would have reason to look back on it as one of their more productive days. Meanwhile, similar groups were hitting the trail behind them nearly every day. Before the first hints of summer filled the air, some fifteen thousand Saints were stretched out across the flat expanse, plodding their way west.

They were following a carefully crafted advance plan, except for one detail: they were a full two months ahead of schedule. They had managed to avoid the worst of the winter snow, although the sleet storms that followed it were almost as effective at making the going rough. And then the rains came. The emigrants endured torrential downpours almost every day for eight straight weeks. Their wagons were soaked and their supplies mildewed. The sheets of rain transformed the prairie into a shallow, muddy lake that strained their horses and oxen. Wagons were often mired hub-deep in the mud and the entire community had to put their shoulders to the wheels to get them moving again. The livestock was already weakened from malnutrition, and the refreshing new grass still didn't show any signs of appearing. Of course, everybody expected all this before they started out, but there was nothing to do but pray for some miracles along the trail. In the meantime they had to keep moving as best they could.

The mud was often as deep as the tops of their boots, and small streams had grown into bottomless cataracts, forcing them to camp on the banks until the water level went down, sometimes after as many as two or three weeks. If there weren't any trees, which was often the case, they couldn't build fires. Without fires they couldn't cook food.

Left: *The Ferry at Council Bluffs, where the first groups of Saints arrived in the middle of June 1846.*

In spite of the hardships these first Mormon migrants faced, they knew that others like them would be following behind, and they did all they could to ease their way by setting up permanent outposts. The first of them was established at Richardson's Point, about fifty miles out from Nauvoo. Like four other such settlements they built farther along the way, it had an established priesthood, a permanent garrison, and stores of firewood and supplies, as well as a blacksmith shop and experienced people who could repair wagons and carts. The first to arrive planted crops, which would be tended by the resident cadre and then harvested by following detachments. In many places simple farms were also cleared to bridge the gaps between the camps.

The most ambitious settlement in the wilderness was Winter Quarters, across from Council Bluffs, Iowa, on the west bank of the Missouri River, the site of the future city of Omaha, Nebraska. It was a small city with about 3,500 people at the beginning, but it eventually harbored large herds of horses and cattle, surrounded by thousands of acres of cultivated land tended by the Saints for the brothers and sisters they knew weren't far behind.

Below: *Winter Quarters was the most ambitious settlement in the wilderness. It provided a supply station for the stream of pilgrims heading west.*

In the later years of the great Mormon exodus, Winter Quarters was abandoned and replaced by a new town called Kanseville on the present-day site of Council Bluffs. It encompassed several smaller winter camps that had been established on the east side of the Missouri River.

The first company reached the Missouri in the middle of June, after a journey that averaged about a hundred miles a month. The last of the Nauvoo refugees, who moved at a slower pace, didn't get there until November. As they prepared to settle in for the winter, word came that three US Army officers were riding up behind, urgently requesting an audience with Brigham Young.

Most of the Saints, weary and discouraged after their eight-month, 400-mile journey through hostile country, believed that it had all come to naught and that the army had been sent to stop them in their tracks, possibly even to slaughter them. But they were mistaken. This was a friendly mission, even if the Saints believed that President James K. Polk was incapable of such a thing.

They were probably right, but the president had embroiled the country in a war with Mexico and now he needed their help. His emissaries requested the services of a battalion of Mormons to help defend California. The Saints were at a crossroads at that moment, divided over plans to move exploratory parties beyond the Missouri to blaze a trail so that other contingents could get further west before winter set in and, possibly, to locate a final site for the New Zion in the Great Basin.

But everything changed after the soldiers arrived. Losing 500 able-bodied men meant that the emigration would have to be put on hold, at least until spring. That in itself may well have saved the Saints from the dangers of winter in the mountains, but there were some other benefits. The government would pay these men for their service, and it would also pick up the bill for their living and travel expenses, a boon to the cash-starved Mormons. Brigham also used the opportunity to secure the government's permission to camp and raise crops on Indian land, which Washington had previously adamantly refused to grant. And he knew that the war was going to put the Basin

Below: *Richard's route of Pioneers. An ornate depiction of the westward route that the travelers must follow.*

EXPLANATION

July, 1847.   ROUTE OF THE MORMON PIONEE

Above: *A monument on the site of Winter Quarters shows a couple enduring the hardships of a prairie winter.*

in American hands, so it would be helpful if the American government happened to be in his debt when it did.

Of course, the decision had a downside as well. Losing 500 of their most able-bodied young men deprived the Saints of strong backs that they desperately needed. Their departure would also add fatherless families to the effort, and others would have to absorb and care for them. Considering these things, Brigham probably wasn't too surprised when his first call for volunteers was met with blank stares. Then he turned the request into an order, thundering that he would draft old men. And if there weren't enough of those, he wouldn't back away from forcing women to join the army. He got his volunteers, forty-one more than he asked for, in fact, but when the so-called Mormon Battalion marched out, whole families marched along with it—women and children and grandfathers, too. Brigham confidently—and accurately, as it turned out—promised them that they weren't likely to see any fighting in California and that they'd all surely come back alive.

But rather than wait for that to happen, he dispatched agents to catch up with them at Fort Leavenworth and collect their clothing allowances, which amounted to about two dollars, and then to follow them on to Santa Fe to be on hand for their first payday. The take there was another $50,000. A government that openly despised the Saints had, almost miraculously, provided them with the funds they desperately needed to get through the winter. As Brigham put it, it had been "a peculiar manifestation of the kind providence of our Heavenly Father."

The main body of Saints spent the winter on the banks of the Missouri, many of them with a roof over their head for the first time since they left Nauvoo more than eight months before. Most of those

FROM NAUVOO TO GREAT SALT LAKE.   Feby, 1846.

roofs were clumps of sod over rough log cabins. Many made their homes in caves, which weren't too bad when compared with life on the move. As one was pleased to point out, there was no danger of being burned out there. But diseases like malaria turned out to be a worse fate than Gentile torches. Death was everywhere that winter. Brigham's son John described it as the "Valley Forge of Mormondom." The emigrants who rode out the storms at the Garden Grove camp, about halfway across Iowa, lost six hundred; men in all of the other camps were kept busy digging graves all winter long. Even at Winter Quarters, the biggest and best-supplied of the camps, the sound of shovels scraping the frozen ground never seemed to stop.

But there was other work to do as well. Winter Quarters had become the nerve center of the Church, from which all the other camps were controlled and worldwide missions monitored. After the money arrived from the Battalion, along with a substantial amount of tithe money from the Saints in England, it was invested in supplies—mostly food—and wagon trains, which were coming and going all through the winter. They acquired more than 30,000 head of cattle and even more sheep, which had to be herded and protected from potential Gentile marauders. They built a gristmill, improved their temporary homes, and worked to prepare themselves for the next leg of their cross-country odyssey into the unknown.

It was an article of faith among all of them that idle hands are the Devil's workshop, but although Brigham kept every pair of hands as busy as he could, there was a disturbing level of dissension in the camp. The weary Saints were all cold and hungry and there was sickness in every

Below: *A photograph of wagons on the trek West. Many such pictures survive.*

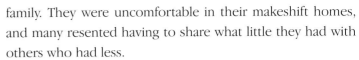

Above: *An oil painting of Winter Quarters shows the size of the growing settlement as more travelers arrived.*

family. They were uncomfortable in their makeshift homes, and many resented having to share what little they had with others who had less.

Brigham responded to their malaise by haranguing them. He was very good at that; it was not for nothing that he was known as the "Lion of the Lord." He told them that if they kept up with this insubordination, they would be "destroyed by the Lamanites, as were the Nephites of old." His preaching drove many of the chastened Saints to repentance and dozens even rushed down to be rebaptized in the icy river.

By the time December turned to January, the influx of new supplies had softened the Saints' resentment and Brigham brought them further from their despair by encouraging them to gather for parties, and even turned the Council House over to them for spontaneous celebrations. "I shall take the liberty of showing you how to dance before the Lord," he promised them. And every day the brass band that had serenaded them along the way lifted their spirits even more.

Brigham and the Apostles spent the winter refining the plan to get to the promised land. Even the most insignificant travelers on the river were questioned about conditions ahead, and their own experience with conditions behind them helped them put it all in perspective. By the time they were on the move again, the Mormon leaders knew exactly where rivers could be forded, which grades they would encounter and how they might handle the steepest of them, and which mountain passes were safest to cross. They knew where Indians might prove to be hostile and where they might find buffalo herds to help restore their food supply. There would be problems along the way, but not very many that they weren't prepared for.

Brigham had pointedly made it known to the Saints that he was not a prophet like Joseph and was not given to receiving heavenly revelations. But once the Twelve had agreed on a plan, he made an exception. He told the faithful that he had received what he characterized as the word and will of the Lord, the only divine inspiration he ever reported having been given.

It was a simple message—the Lord would not expect anything more from the Saints than they were capable of accomplishing. He said that they should continue organizing into companies as before, and that each of them should poll its membership to find out how many could afford to make the journey. They were also to take as many of the poor, including the families of Battalion members, as they were able to feed and outfit. And they were expected to supply and house those who would have to be left behind. Brigham's revelation ended with an exhortation to the Saints to pay their debts, maintain their testimony of the faith, humble themselves, and stop drinking. He also reminded them of past tribulations and warned them of certain destruction if their faith should fail.

Chapter 6
The Place of Refuge

Above: All is well along the Platte River, the next phase of the journey.

The date of their departure from Winter Quarters was set for April 6, 1847, the anniversary of the day seventeen years earlier when Joseph Smith and Oliver Cowdery became the Church's first Elders. They moved out in waves and rendezvoused on the banks of the Elkhorn River about twenty miles away. When they left there together ten days later, the ranks of the pioneer company were made up of three women, two children, and 143 men, including eight Apostles and eighteen high priests. Their train was composed of seventy-three wagons, ninety-three horses, and fifty-two mules. It was followed by a herd of nineteen cows kept on their best behavior by seventeen dogs. A flock of chickens brought up the rear. Ten more similar companies followed them in the early summer, bringing the number on the trail west of the Missouri River to more than 1,800.

When they reached the Platte River a little further on, they set their course along its north bank, establishing a route that became known as the Mormon Trail. They knew that there would be more grass for their livestock on that side, and they also knew that Gentile wagon trains usually followed the south bank. Those other emigrants had enough problems of their own, but the Mormons never lost their terror of being attacked by them.

Parley Pratt had brought back navigation instruments from his missionary trips to England, and his brother, the Apostle Orson Pratt, put them to good use keeping track of their exact location as they

Above: *Mountain man Jim Bridger gave the pioneers advice to help them reach Salt Lake City, which he described as a "paradise."*

Below: *Small tents provided some shelter in the harsh environment along the trail. The camp here is at the Elkhorn River, just west of Winter Quarters.*

moved along. He and others also collected observations on the terrain and they were able to create the most accurate maps that had yet been drawn of the region they passed through. Along with their detailed descriptions, the maps were published the following year in a guidebook to ease the way for future contingents of Saints. Apostle Pratt also invented a device that counted the rotations of a wagon wheel and made it possible for him to compute the number of miles they traveled. Others used the information to create logbooks that were deposited in slotted boards at regular intervals for the following companies, and also served as mile posts for Gentile wagon trains following the Oregon Trail. The messages they left behind invariably ended with the words "All is well!"

Indeed, everything seemed to be going quite well during the first weeks of their march. They functioned with strict military precision and, of course, they all believed that they were being guided and protected by the will of the Lord. The fact is, they seemed to be having too much fun. At least Brigham thought so. Agitated by the frivolity of card-playing, dancing, and horseplay, he called the procession to a halt at Scott's Bluff and read them the riot act.

"I do not feel like going any further with this company of men and with the spirit that now prevails in this camp," he railed. "If anyone shall attempt to introduce anything that is unlawful . . . I swear they shall not return home." The tirade ended and the priests among them put on their robes and went into the woods to pray. The frivolity came to an abrupt end, although Brigham's own initial charge to them had been to "be happy and show your gratitude in music, dance and prayer." The problem was that there had been too much of the former and not enough of the latter.

A few days later, they crossed over to Fort Laramie to repair their

Above: *The first pioneer wagon trains arriving at Echo Canyon, as they descend the mountains into the Great Salt Lake Valley.*

wagons and to get valuable information from other parties passing through. Some of those were the feared Gentiles from Missouri, always a hotbed of anti-Mormonism, but, wonder of wonders, they all turned out to be helpful and friendly. As far as the Saints were concerned, though, this was probably just a sign of a secret plot to put them off their guard. But they chose to regard it as a sign from the Lord that He would protect them.

Something even more wonderful happened when they reached the fords crossing the Platte: they found a way to get the Gentiles to help finance their journey. As if by a miracle (and who could deny it?), heavy rains had made it necessary for them to make the crossing on barges. Gentile wagons were backed up, waiting for the water to subside. Once they had gotten themselves across, the Saints went back and offered the use of their boats for fees that were usually paid in much-needed food. The ferry service was so successful that they built a blacksmith shop on the riverbank to turn another profit repairing Gentile wagons. Brigham was so impressed by all this that he left a few men behind to run the operation, and of course, he left them with an appropriate schedule of fees.

Their route along the North Platte River from Fort Laramie to Fort

Bridger followed the well-traveled Oregon Trail. It was on that leg that they spotted the landmarks that guided all of the westbound American emigrants—Independence Rock and the Sweetwater River. And it was where they first saw the Wind River Mountains off in the distance.

The Pioneers crossed the Continental Divide at South Pass, where Brigham stopped to get fresh information from a trader going the other way. He brought news of Sam Brannan's Mormon settlement in California's San Joaquin Valley, as well as a report of his own recent reconnaissance in the Salt Lake Basin. His warnings that they were headed into hostile country were welcome, and even respected, although they already knew what to expect. But Brigham's mind was made up and he opted to go there and see for himself.

As the pioneers were moving down from South Pass, they met up with Jim Bridger, also known as Old Gabe, a legendary mountain man who had spent his boyhood down in the Great Basin and probably knew more about it than any man alive. He had gone back to live there by then as it turned out, operating a fortified trading post about a hundred miles east of the Great Salt Lake.

During a day-long round of conversations, Bridger filled them in on every small detail of what he called a "paradise." He told them about the trees they'd find there, the minerals waiting to be mined, the roots that were edible, the best places to look for a town site, and most of all, what to expect from the local Indians. These pitiful Paiutes, he said, could be driven out in less than twenty-four hours, although in his opinion it might be better to let them stay and use them as slaves. Of course, Old Gabe had spent most of his life among the hostile tribes in the northern Rockies, so his opinion might well have been taken with a grain of salt.

At that point, Brigham was still undecided about where the Saints should actually settle in the Great Basin. He was considering both the Salt Lake Valley and the territory around Utah Lake to its south. Bridger's advice probably tipped the decision for the more northerly site, although he had cautioned that it might be a tough job growing grain there. Bridger backed up the warning with a bet, offering to pay a thousand dollars to the first farmer who could produce a bushel of corn on that land. But he also warned Brigham that the Indians to the south were hostile and could cause no end of trouble.

But the Saints weren't there quite yet. When they were within striking distance of their goal at the Green River, mountain fever broke out in the camp, and it eventually afflicted Brigham himself. He was too weak to move when the pioneers started to scout the territory ahead. They didn't have much farther to go, but it would turn out to involve the most grueling miles of their whole journey.

The well-traveled Oregon Trail turned to the northwest at the Green River, but the pioneer company of Mormons continued westward into the forbidding Wasatch Mountains. The range is one of the most

Wagon Trains

The Mormon pioneers were remarkably self-sufficient, trusting only in God and their own skills to guide them on their trek across the prairies and mountains. Unfortunately, fear of interference and persecution had made them wary of their fellow Americans, and they took care to avoid the trails used by the Gentiles' wagon trains. This policy led them to a trail on the north bank of the Platte River, because Gentile immigrants used the one on the south bank. Luckily, this route proved to be rich in pasture for their livestock, and it became known as the Mormon Trail.

A wagon train consisted of, on average, seventy-three wagons, 143 men, three women, two children, ninety-three horses, and fifty-two mules, followed by nineteen cows, seventeen dogs, and a flock of chickens.

Early wagon train leaders surveyed the route and passed on accurate maps and observations of the terrain to those that followed. The industrious Mormon pioneers managed to make a business from helping those that followed, such as offering ferry services across the swollen Platte River. They charged an appropriate schedule of fees in order to pay for much-needed supplies.

The sheer logistics of transporting large numbers of people, along with their personal effects, across great distances was daunting. Constant repairs were required to keep the wagons rolling, the design of which had hardly changed since the Middle Ages. Wooden spokes would break over the rocky tracks, metal tires became loose in the scorching summer heat, hubs would split, and harnesses would fray. All things considered, it was a minor miracle that anything survived the journey intact. Many skills that had been learned establishing the settlements at Kirtland and Nauvoo now came to the fore.

beautiful of the Rocky Mountains, but frustrating, with small, twisting canyons that more often than not led nowhere. The explorers managed to find one rocky gap—now called Emigrant Canyon—that did have an outlet. They threaded their way through it, but always with the feeling that there had to be a better way, even though they knew that there probably wasn't. In their report on the exploration, the men wrote that, "it is uncertain whether man or beast ever trod [through the Canyon] before, unless it be a bear or a rattlesnake."

They were wrong though. Humans had come this way before. It was the route that had been used by the ill-fated Donner party looking for a shortcut to California the previous summer, and the explorers found the road they had built to get their wagons over the Wasatch. But they also found it overgrown and impassable, and it took them more than two weeks to clear the brush, pry boulders loose, cut trees, and regrade the right-of-way.

Their leader, the ubiquitous Orson Pratt, became the first to actually see the promised land. On July 19, he scouted a high mountain ridge from which he said he could see "an extensive level prairie some few miles distant, which we thought must be near the lake." Two days later, in the company of Erastus Snow, Pratt got a better view from the top of Little Mountain, where they "looked out on the full extent of the valley where the waters of the Great Salt Lake glistened in the sunbeams." He added that, "we could not refrain from the shout of joy which almost involuntarily escaped from our lips."

In another two nights, the entire company, except for those who had stayed behind to tend to their afflicted leader, finally camped together in the land of Canaan for the first time. But being Mormons, this

Above: *Lithograph of trail life.*

wasn't a time for rest and rejoicing. They were divided into committees to get on with the job of putting crops into the ground, and they began plowing almost as soon as they gathered. While the soil appeared to be rich enough to sustain crops, it was also painfully dry, so they built a dam for irrigation before the sun went down.

Though this was the promised land, the land itself didn't seem very promising. Except for clumps of sage, nothing was growing there but stunted oak trees. There was thick alkali dust covering everything, the sun beat down mercilessly, and the only sign of life was an

Above: *The first waves of pioneers entering the Great Salt Lake Valley.*

unusually large number of crickets and rattlesnakes. What it was, was a desert. But the Saints were grateful for it. No one had told them that life was going to be easy out here, and no one loves a challenge more than a Latter-day Saint.

The remembered day of deliverance is the following day: July 24, 1847. Early that afternoon, a small caravan of canvas-topped wagons managed to make it over the still-torturous road. In the midst of them was a carriage with the still-weak Brigham Young lying in back. He had little to say, except, "This is the place." And as if to confirm it, the Lord sent a rain shower, which the gathered Saints all knew was a rare event in these parts.

Writing in his journal, Young noted, "We were on the spot where the city was to be built and I knew it as the place I had seen in my vision and we might explore the mountains over and over again and each time return to this place as the best." The first phase of the exodus was over, but the work had barely begun.

Chapter 7

Greater Glory

Although Brigham had told them that the place had been found, the Saints divided themselves into exploring committees to see if they might find a better one. They couldn't, and a few days later Brigham designated the spot where the temple should be built and presented his plans for the new city of Zion, closely based on Joseph's plan for Kirtland, which had more or less been duplicated at Nauvoo.

The mountain fever he had contracted left burning pain in his swollen joints, but Brigham had more work to do. Just a few weeks later, after supervising the early construction, he and a company of men began retracing the trail back to Winter Quarters to bring in the rest of the Saints who were scattered in the way stations strung out across the prairie. At various points along the way, they met the ten companies that had followed them out of Winter Quarters. They

Below: The last but toughest part of the journey.

carried many more people than Brigham had planned for, and he felt that his orders had been disobeyed. But he understood their eagerness and let them move on to their new home. It was only the beginning. About 62,000 more would follow over the next twenty years in what would be remembered as the Mormon Trek.

Other Americans who went west in the 1840s were generally bound for Oregon or California, and they were responding to what they believed was their Manifest Destiny, a concept put forward in a newspaper editorial endorsing Democrat James K. Polk for the presidency in 1844, and which came to be interpreted by most Americans as an expression of their mandate from God to plant their superior institutions and virtues out in those wide, open spaces. The Mormons believed that God was leading them westward too, but theirs was a distinctly different call. As far as the Mormons were concerned, their journey was nothing more or less than a response to the covenant God had made with Moses as he began to lead the Israelites out of Egypt: "For thou art an holy people unto the Lord thy God." Just as He had delivered the ancient tribes of Israel out of bondage and protected them in the wilderness, now in these latter days He was once again leading His chosen people to the promised land. It was clearly a fulfillment of the prophecy of the Lord delivered by Isaiah, "And I will bring forth a seed out of Jacob, and out of Judah an inheritor of my mountains: and mine elect shall inherit it, and my servants shall dwell there."

And now that they were finally beyond the reach of their enemies, the Latter-day Saints would establish a new kingdom of Zion near the shores of the Great Salt Lake. Brigham named it "Deseret," which the Book of Mormon defines as the "land of the honey bee," symbolic of industry. He claimed all of the territory out from the basin as far west as California, south to Mexico, and north into Wyoming as part of it. The government would eventually disabuse him of that idea by creating the much smaller Territory of Utah. But no matter what it was called, it was still the undisputed territory of the Mormons, and they were willing, even eager, to take on the backbreaking job of turning a worthless desert into a land of true promise. It had always been their special destiny.

The first adobe houses in the new Mormon city were clustered together inside a fort with a cattle yard at its center. Brigham had recommended that the yard be plowed in the spring to create gardens that were to be equally divided among all the families, who would then

Above: *An early lithograph of pioneers crossing the mountains, with a depiction of Brigham Young inset. It was Young who had masterminded the exodus.*

be able to raise crops inside the fort's protective walls. He ordered that nearby City Creek should be diverted to bring water to these gardens and surround the stockade to water the pasture land on the outside.

At the time he crafted his plan, Brigham believed that the city would accommodate about a hundred families, but allowing for wagon trains that were already on their way from Winter Quarters,that would swell the number by another 400 families or more, what had been planned as an efficient community of fewer than 500 Saints had to be quickly expanded to take care of four times that many, not to mention the 5,000 head of cattle they were bringing along with them.

The problem was solved by building two more forts connected to the original one and clearing more space outside for the livestock and for planting more garden plots, as well as digging the irrigation ditches that would be needed to water them.

The Saints made it all look easy, but there were a few problems, of course. Among them were disputes over the land distribution; some believed that the fort had been built in the wrong place and others felt that too much was being asked of them in the way of enforced community labor at a time when they all had their hands full providing for their own families. But the goal of establishing this kingdom had always been to put a safe distance between themselves and the hostile Gentiles, and that left them out on their own with no

Below: *The Great Salt Lake spreads out below, the first glimpse for many of the New Zion.*

one but each other to turn to for aid and comfort. The only way to survive this far from civilization was through mutual cooperation, and it was a rare Saint who didn't realize that.

Every organized community of people, from the ancients of the Tigris River Valley to the modern Israelis, has known very well that the only way to secure a claim to the land is to create settlements on it. The Mormons were well aware that their City of Refuge wasn't enough to secure their position, and even as they were surveying the center, other town sites were being scouted in the area. They began moving out into them near the end of their first year in the valley. The first moves were to the north, where small communities were built along nearly every creek below the Weber River, which itself became the site of a larger town they called Brownsville, later to be know as Ogden. Others moved to the south, where they secured permission from the Ute Indians to establish forts and town sites. Land in all of these places was to be distributed free to newcomers, and the existence of the settlements guaranteed that none of them would wind up homeless.

Food had become desperately short even before their first

winter in the valley finally ended, but when the spring sun started to ripen the wheat that they had planted when they first arrived, hope sprouted along with it. The warm sun brought life to the vegetables they'd planted, and thick, lush blossoms on their fruit trees gave them an assurance that they could expect to have a good harvest. But then all their hopes disappeared in what could only be compared to the biblical plague of locusts. Wave after wave of huge black crickets, some remembered as being as big as mice, suddenly appeared out of nowhere, devouring every green thing in their path. The Saints fought back, swatting them with sticks and boards and water-soaked rags, but still the hordes kept coming. They tried drowning them by diverting water from the irrigation ditches, but the water was quickly filled with dead insects and live ones used them as bridges to avoid drowning themselves. There didn't seem to be any way to hold back this terrible tide and, with it, certain

Below: *A painting depicts the miracle of the seagulls. This was a significant event in the founding years of Salt Lake City.*

"GATHERING TO ZION"—LIFE BY THE WAY.

Above: *Wagons and handcarts required constant repair as this picture shows. We can only hope that they had something decent to eat after a hard day on the trail, followed by hours of wheel fixing.*

ruination of all of their crops and their hopes along with them—except through prayer.

The entire community was on its knees when the sky darkened again. This time it was flocks of seagulls flying in from the lake, although few of the Saints regarded it as anything like an answer to their prayers—these birds were crop eaters. But on this occasion, the gulls had an appetite only for crickets and they devoured them by the thousands over the next few weeks. Finally, when there were no crickets left, the gulls flew off west toward their nests on the islands in the lake fifteen miles away. A miracle? Probably. At least the Saints were convinced that they had just witnessed one—and they were about to experience another.

Though their crops had been decimated, they were still able to salvage enough to make it through their second winter in the valley, although many were on the edge of starvation by the time spring came around again. They knew that in time the land would deliver up its bounty once more. However, the practical among them knew that wouldn't happen before July at the earliest, and few of them were confident that they wouldn't starve to death before then. While they were short of food, they were also short of cash to buy more, but they had faith that God would provide. And He did, in a most unexpected way.

Among the earliest visitors to the new city was Sam Brannan, the man who had established the Mormon colony in California. Some of the men from the Mormon Battalion who had wound up there after the end of the Mexican War sent word with him, asking Brigham what they should do next, and his advice to them was to stay where they were, find jobs, save their money, and wait for word to come home to the Salt Lake Valley.

Most of them took the advice and some went to work for John

Left: *Panning for gold during the Gold Rush of the 1840s. Brigham Young encouraged the Saints to stay at home. In fact, they managed to profit by doing so. Most of the forty-niners passed through Salt Lake City on their way to the goldfields and generated enormous trading opportunities.*

Marshall, who ran a sawmill on land owned by John Sutter on the American River, east of San Francisco. In January 1848, as the Saints were struggling to survive their first winter at Deseret, one of those men, Henry Bigler, wrote in his journal, "Some kind of metal was found in the tail race that looks like gold." Marshall swore him to secrecy, but he shared the secret with Brannan, who let the cat out of the bag with an article that ran in the Mormon newspaper, *The California Star*, under the headline "Gold! Gold! Gold!" Other publications enthusiastically relayed the message across the country and the California Gold Rush of 1849 was inevitable.

Brigham Young firmly discouraged the Saints from going off to the goldfields themselves, warning them of the harm that the lust for mammon would surely bring to their souls. But as it happened, there was no need for them to leave their homes to be able to reap the benefits of gold fever.

There were several different ways to get from the East Coast to California, but the fastest and most direct of them was a southern route that ran right through Salt Lake City. The first to pass that way was a wagon train made up of hardware and dry-goods wholesalers off to make a killing in the mining camps. But when word reached them that their competitors had already beaten them to California, they decided not to throw good money after bad and sold their goods to the Saints at depressed prices rather than haul the freight the rest of the way only to face an even bigger loss.

The first waves of forty-niners began passing through not long afterward, and they were crestfallen to learn that after the long slog to get this far, they were still 700 miles short of the gold they were after. Many of them traded their big wagons for smaller ones that would be easier to get across the mountains and deserts ahead, and every time they did, the Mormons got the better of the bargain. It's easy to imagine how the Saints might have exaggerated the dangers out there. It was good business, after all.

Some of the travelers didn't bother trading their goods and simply discarded the supplies they had been carrying and set off to finish the trip on horseback. In these cases, the Saints won both ends of the bargain. Not only did they get to keep the abandoned supplies, but they were pleased to be able to engage in a little horse trading, swapping well-fed horses for the half-starved nags that had carried these would-be prospectors from the East. Time and care would restore them to enough vigor to make them valuable trades for future travelers.

The fact is, the Mormons were willing to make trades for just about anything that the forty-niners were willing to part with. What the travelers didn't know was that they were dealing with what may have been the slickest traders in North America. Barter had been their basic means of survival since Joseph Smith first led them out of upstate New York, and they had become very good at it.

The result of all this wheeling and dealing was that before very long, Salt Lake City was transformed into one of the most prosperous little towns in the West. It even had its own mint to produce gold coins from the bags of dust that successful prospectors used to buy provisions when they passed through on their way back home. There

Below: A modern re-creation of a Deseret street scene.

was no more talk—and no more fear—of imminent starvation. Another miracle? Who can say? But it would have been impossible to find a Saint who didn't believe that it was.

The fruit of that second Mormon miracle was civic improvement. Mark Twain, who didn't mind telling anyone how much he despised Mormons (he was a Missourian, after all), visited there in the 1860s and recorded his impressions in his book *Roughing It*. He described the Salt Lake Valley as "a fairy-land to us, to all intents and purposes, a land of enchantment, and goblins, and awful mystery." After visiting Salt Lake City itself, he reported:

> We strolled about everywhere through the broad, straight, level streets, and enjoyed the pleasant strangeness of a city of fifteen-thousand inhabitants with no loafers perceptible in it; and no visible drunkards or noisy people; a limpid stream rippling and dancing through every street in place of a filthy gutter; block after block of trim dwellings, built of

Above: *Beehive House, one of two Brigham Young residences in downtown Salt Lake City. It was named for the beehive sculpture on the roof, which symbolized industriousness.*

[wood] frame or sunburned brick—a great thriving orchard behind every one of them, apparently—branches from the street streams winding and sparkling among the garden beds and fruit trees, and a grand general air of neatness, repair, thrift and comfort around and about and over the whole. And everywhere were workshops, factories, and all manner of industries; and intent faces and busy hands were to be seen wherever one looked; and in one's ears was the ceaseless clink of hammers, the buzz of trade and the contented hum of drums and flywheels."

Possibly because of his low opinion of Latter-day Saints, Mark

Twain never mentioned the Salt Lake Tabernacle, which was the city's showplace even then, even though it was still in the early stages of construction when he passed through. Work had begun in 1853, and it was dedicated forty years later. In the city's early years, the ten-acre site, known from the beginning as Temple Square, had been surrounded by an eight-foot-tall brick wall that enclosed an open-air meeting place called the Bowery, which was protected from the sun by tree branches spread out over wooden frames. Though services were held there, it was a long way from being a proper temple. While they waited for one to be built, the Saints erected a nearby "Endowment House," where temple rituals could be performed.

For all intents and purposes, early Salt Lake City very much resembled the cities back East. Apart from its majestic setting, the most striking difference was the width of its streets, the main ones being 125 feet across. By way of comparison, the broad avenues in Manhattan are only a hundred feet wide between building lines. The irrigation canals that impressed Mark Twain were watched over by an appointed water master, whose job was to make sure that every property owner received a predetermined share of the life-giving water, without which the city would still have been a desert. The same was true out on the farms, with water being carefully rationed according to need. In most places, it was distributed to different farmers on alternate days and within prescribed hours, much in the same way that modern cities mandate when lawns can be watered and when they cannot.

The houses were all similar, plain, two-story structures that differed from their neighbors only in the materials used to build them. Most were adobe, some were fired clay brick, and the more affluent brought wood down from the mountains to impress their neighbors. Among these was Brigham's mansion, called the Beehive House because he had placed a gilded representation of a beehive on a parapet above the roof as a constant reminder of the industriousness he demanded of all of the Saints.

Brigham Young had all the attributes of a tycoon, and among the businesses he owned and ran—a long list of enterprises that included the city's only hotel—was a sawmill in the nearby mountains. So it was only natural that the house he personally built for himself should be with lumber from his own mill. The subtle message was "go ye and do likewise," but there were other reasons why he had the biggest and grandest house in the city. He had been named President and Prophet of the Church after they gathered there, becoming the sole heir to the authority of Joseph Smith, and the house was, in effect, an executive mansion. Besides, he also had fifty-seven children and he must have needed the space.

The Early Days in Salt Lake City

These photographs clearly show how the settlement at Salt Lake bore many of the hallmarks of previous Mormon settlements. Like Kirtland and Nauvoo, the growing city was laid out with wide streets and substantial buildings in stone, brick, and wood. This resulted in a city that resembled those back east, and it was a stark contrast to the usual "cow town" architecture of the West. Trees were planted for shade, and this tradition continues. The "greening" campaign of 2000 was established to increase the amount of green space in downtown Salt Lake City. As always, the centerpiece of the city was to be the Temple, and work began on the building in Temple Square as early as 1853.

The city layout also incorporated irrigation canals in its basic design to ensure that gardens, orchards, and shade trees could all thrive. Using these techniques meant that the early Mormons were indeed able to make a green place in the desert.

Chapter 8
Wars and Deliverance

Opposite page, right: *Brigham Young became the sole heir to Joseph Smith's authority as President and Prophet of the Mormon people. He oversaw the development of both Church doctrine and the settling of the Utah territory.*

Congress designated Utah a territory in 1851 and made Brigham Young its territorial governor, as well as giving him the job of Supervisor of Indian Affairs. Washington also appointed Mormons almost exclusively to run the government and appropriated funds to pay their salaries and to cover the expenses of their offices.

But as far as most of the Saints were concerned, it was still Deseret. Although they welcomed the influx of federal money, not much changed in the way they governed themselves. Contrary to the Constitution, church and state were thoroughly and inexorably intertwined here. Over the previous two years, they had carved out counties and towns, passed laws to protect natural resources, regulated trade, and reorganized the Nauvoo Legion as their protectors, all of it accomplished through the authority of the Church. They had long since anointed Brigham Young as their governor, and his close associates in the Church leadership were chosen to head the various departments that they felt would be necessary to a proper government. All of the other important public offices were held by members of the Council of Fifty, and bishops in each ward were appointed magistrates of the probate courts.

Brigham seemed to be the perfect choice to handle Indian affairs. No leader in the early West had dealt with the problem with as much fairness and understanding. In fact, no other leader in the history of America, except possibly the Quaker William Penn, has ever demonstrated the same respect for the people who were there first.

When the Saints first arrived in the Great Basin, more than 20,000 Indians were already living there, and the first of them showed up on missions to trade for guns and clothing even before the first buildings went up. Over time, more of them came more often. But when fighting broke out between two competing bands, Brigham ordered that trading could only be done at the Indian villages, and he designated special agents as the only valid traders. The relationship turned nasty a bit later when the natives began attacking outlying farms and threatened to mount an all-out attack on Fort Utah on the Provo River. When the militia responded and some forty Indians were killed in the two-day battle, the local tribes, who weren't very warlike to begin with, backed off and never threatened the white settlements and farms again. But that was more a result of Brigham Young's

diplomacy than any fear of more bloodshed.

Brigham had always preached tolerance for the Native Americans. "They are the seed of Abraham, and our God is ever their God," he said. He believed that a policy of peace was the cheapest option; "it is preferable to feed them than to fight them." It would take more than a generation for the US government to get that message.

After the skirmish at Fort Utah, Ute Chief Wakara led his people off to the safety of the mountains, and the soldiers ached to follow them and remove the threat once and for all. But Brigham refused to let them go. Instead he wrote a letter to the chief, enclosed in a package of tobacco that he invited him to smoke "when you get lonesome."

"You are a fool for fighting your best friends," he wrote, "for we are your best friends, and the only friends you have in the world. Everybody else will kill you if they could get a chance. If you get hungry send some friendly Indians down to the settlements and we will give you some beef cattle and flour. When you get good-natured again, I would like to see you. Don't you think you should be ashamed? You know I have always been your best friend." The Indians ceased to be a problem to the Mormons on that day. They were more eager for friendly trade, and some were even baptized into the Church. They were very much impressed by the fact that the story of their ancestors played such a large role in the Book of Mormon, and they were even more impressed by the kindness of the Saints themselves. It was a sharp contrast to the attitude of the other white men they had seen. But peace with the Indians presented Brigham with a problem. Or rather, part of a larger one.

When he first saw the Great Basin, Brigham said, "Give us ten years in this valley and we will ask no odds of Uncle Sam or the devil."

But after the ten years had passed, he was beginning to think that the devil was hard at work in their midst, and he had a nagging feeling that Uncle Sam was going to bring trouble down on them again.

The Mormons thrived beyond their wildest imaginings in that first decade. They had made the desert blossom, they were nearly all prosperous, the Indians were no longer a threat, and the Gentiles were a safe distance away. But Brigham believed that these things had begun to make them complacent. He told them, "We are the happiest people when we have what are called trials, for then the spirit of God is more abundantly bestowed upon the faithful."

But the message was lost on the younger members of his audience. They themselves hadn't experienced the pain of persecution, and their parents had let it vanish from their own memories. Apart from that, most of these people were happier than they had ever been in their lives. They may have asked themselves, "Who needs more trial and tribulation?" And Brigham might have answered them, "You do."

The problem, as he saw it, was that they were losing their moral values and that they were in grave danger of falling into a rut along the road to perfection, a Saint's primary reason for an earthly life. If he needed proof that this was so, his bishop-magistrates could have provided it. Petty thievery was filling their court calendars, and so was silly feuding between families. It all seemed inconsequential, but taken together, there was a pattern there and Brigham Young knew it.

Old-fashioned revivalism had reasserted itself back east by that time, especially in the Southern States, and one of the great masters of its preaching style was Jedediah Grant, a Mormon missionary. After he relocated to Salt Lake City, he rose quickly among the Church's leadership and took the city virtually by storm with his fiery sermons. It was revivalism, pure and simple, but instead of bringing converts forward to receive Christ into their lives, Grant led them outdoors for rebaptism into the faith of the Church of Jesus Christ of Latter-day Saints.

Although Joseph Smith, and Brigham Young after him, had condemned the practices of the revivalists as shallow, Brigham was impressed by this means of dealing with complacency among the pious, and it led him to announce a new Church policy. He didn't call it "revivalism," but rather "Reformation." He based it not on fiery preaching, but rather on a program of self-examination within family units. Missionaries were sent from door to door in each ward with a list of questions to be asked of every family member. More often than not, families continued the discussions after the missionary left, and the plan seemed to work quite well. As one Apostle explained, "[It] has been a mirror to the Saints, reflecting themselves in truth."

Among the side effects of these one-on-one meetings were the discovery of illness and poverty among some families who were too proud to ask for help, and that exposed Church leaders who should have been aware of such things, but hadn't bothered to do anything about them. Many of them were relieved of their responsibility and in some cases they were replaced by others who had participated in the self-study of the Reformation.

The movement was short-lived and it was controversial. In their zealous response, some of the Saints felt secure enough in their faith to forget about public animosity and felt free to tell outsiders of such previously unknown concepts as blood atonement, tied to Christ's atonement by shedding His blood as a sacrifice for the Original Sin. It wasn't a doctrine of the Mormon Church, but was sometimes used as a reminder to the Saints of the seriousness of crimes such as murder. The Old Testament had told them that if any man should kill an innocent person, "by men shall his blood be shed."

Enemies of the Church twisted the idea and charged that ritual executions were taking place in the Mormon camp, but none of them offered anything in the way of proof. Still, it was the seed of a rumor that was told and retold in every part of the country. These wild tales horrified outsiders, in spite of the fact that they themselves equated public hangings with public entertainment and regarded a lynching as a grand excuse for a picnic. Then there were those old rumors about polygamy. Although the Mormons were safely out of the reach of the Gentiles, their enemies were starting to claw at the gates again.

The pot began to simmer when one of the federal judges assigned to the territory went to the Bowery to accept a block of Utah granite for the new Washington Monument and turned the occasion into an opportunity to vent his spleen on Brigham Young and the Saints. He began by haranguing the Governor for his recent unkind remarks about the late President Zachary Taylor, to which Brigham responded by saying, "Zachary Taylor is dead and gone to hell, and I'm glad of it."

Next the judge turned his attention to the women in the audience. He wagged his finger at them and solemnly warned, "You must become virtuous, and teach your daughters to become virtuous, or your offering [the block of stone] had better remain in the bosom of your native mountains."

When it was his turn to speak, Brigham addressed the judge as an "illiterate ranter," and coldly informed him that there were no women anywhere more virtuous than Mormon women. Then he told him to get out of the territory, "the sooner the better."

After that, the Mormon community completely shunned the three federal judges who had been appointed to serve them. Considering the demographics in the Utah Territory at that time, it left them with no one to socialize with except each other. About a month later, they all packed their bags and caught the next stagecoach headed in the general direction of Washington. They left the block of granite behind, but carried off the funds that had been sent to run their courts.

In the inevitable press conferences that followed, the judges asserted that Utah was the wildest and most lawless place anywhere in the Wild West, and they claimed that they had been forced to leave it because their lives had been threatened. They also told the world that they could prove once and for all that polygamy was rampant out there. But Brigham had beaten them to the punch by revealing that fact himself while they were still making their bumpy way back home. It took the wind out of their sails, but it didn't settle the question.

Even though he carefully explained why the practice had been instituted, Brigham's words didn't have any impact at all on American public opinion. The rumor mill saw to that. There was serious talk of arresting the Mormon leaders for violating the Constitution, even though it doesn't mention plural marriage. The Saints responded that they were protected by that same Constitution's provision of freedom of religion. These practices that so offended their fellow Americans were their right as expressions of religious ideas and freedom of faith, they argued. Naturally, most of their fellow Americans didn't buy into that and the rumors only got nastier.

Brigham's term as governor wasn't renewed when it expired, but he

Below: *James Buchanan, the fifteenth president of the United States, sent a contingent of 2,500 armed troops to Utah in an attempt to bring the territory under the control of central government.*

just carried on as though he were still endowed with a federal mandate, even if his paychecks stopped coming. No one in the federal bureaucracy wanted the job anyway, but one thing was certain—almost no one back east wanted Brigham Young left in charge either.

The new president, James Buchanan, took the bull by the horns and appointed a man named Alfred Cumming as Utah's new territorial governor. Buchanan was blindsided by scores of spurious intelligence reports asserting that the Mormons were totally under Brigham's thumb and that they had nothing but contempt for Congress and its laws. One report even told him, although it doesn't seem to have been true, that a secret society had been established in their midst to use force to resist federal authority. Buchanan had heard all the other anti-Mormon rumors, and he decided it would be wise to send a contingent of 2,500 armed troops to facilitate Cumming's entry into this hornet's nest disguised as a beehive.

In his wisdom, the president had neglected to let Brigham know that the troops were on the way or why he had issued the order in the first place. When he found out about it, the Mormon leader concluded that he was left with no choice but to meet force with force. The Saints had been attacked in this way too many times before and they had no intention of being driven from their homes at gunpoint again.

Word of the troop assembly had come from Mormon agents at Fort Laramie in July, but troops moved slowly in those days, and the column didn't reach sight of the valley until September. The leader of the vanguard, Captain Stewart Van Vliet, was dumbfounded when he learned that his men were being regarded as invaders. As far as he knew, his job was just to show the flag and ease the way for the new governor, and he was there in advance of the troops to buy supplies and arrange billeting for them. It seemed that everyone had gone mad.

The captain quickly came to the realization that this was all the result of a colossal misunderstanding. But though the Mormons treated him respectfully, they let him know in no uncertain terms that he and his men were facing a bloody battle, and nothing he could say would prevent it.

Van Vliet's report to his commander was that the Mormons intended to burn their houses and crops, tear up their roads, smash their dams, and turn Utah back into a desert if the troops kept coming. Then they would stampede their cattle into the path of the approaching army and retreat into the mountains, girded for a long guerrilla war.

This was no fantasy dreamed up by a panicky soldier, but an awful truth. Brigham had already declared martial law and had issued a formal declaration ordering the Saints to leave nothing behind them that could be of use to the invading army and to "waste away our enemies and lose none." Brigham Young never said anything he didn't mean.

In the midst of all this turmoil and uncertainty, an incident 200 miles to the south stirred more animosity against the Mormons than almost anything that had ever gone before.

In the fall season, California-bound wagon trains often passed through southern Utah to avoid mountain snows, and the first of this season was the so-called Francher party, which preferred to be known as the Missouri Wildcats. It was rumored that some of them were bragging about having taken part in the Mormon massacres in their home territory, and wouldn't mind tasting blood again.

Meanwhile, the Indians felt that the protection of the Mormons gave them license to attack wagon trains like these, and when this first one of the season camped at Mountain Meadow, the braves went on the warpath. After a long siege, the Mormon militia arrived on the scene, assuming, rightly or wrongly, that their mission was to wipe out the Francher company, although they let the Indians actually do the job and take the blame. Their part in it was to lure the besieged

Missourians out of their camp. When they did, the Indians attacked in force; 121 people were killed and only about twenty children escaped death.

Brigham was told that it had been an Indian massacre and nothing more. But little by little, the facts started coming out and the local leaders who had taken part in the Mountain Meadow incident were relieved of their responsibilities. A Mormon farmer named John Lee, who admitted to his part in it, was executed for his crime years later, but none of the others ever stood trial.

The horror of the event was front-page news for days, and every word of every story was like a nail being pounded into the coffin of the Church of Jesus Christ of Latter-day Saints, even though the Church had nothing to do with it apart from the fact that some of its members were involved. It was all a misunderstanding—just like the ugly situation to the north as US troops were still marching toward Utah.

The leader of that army, General Albert Sidney Johnston, had been detained on other business, and he didn't catch up with his men until it was too late to reach Utah before the winter snows started blowing in. His men had been moving on without him, but the Nauvoo Legion was ready for them. The militiamen built stone walls and sniper trenches in Echo Canyon, the most likely route into Salt Lake City, and more than a thousand of them were dug in, waiting for the invasion. They had also loosened boulders to use as missiles, and they dug channels below dams that could be knocked away to flood the pass.

When General Johnston finally arrived on the scene, he ordered his troops to march instead to Fort Bridger to hole-up for the winter. By the time they got to the fort though, the Mormons had already been there and had burned all of the wooden buildings, leaving them with only stone shells of foundations for shelter. The troops managed to survive the harshness of the situation, and except for minor attacks on their supply trains, the Utah War turned out to be a bloodless one.

Newspapers back east considered any Mormon story hot copy, and their reports of the gathering war clouds were about as hot as any could be. None of them had any reporters anywhere near the scene of the action, but relied instead on reports published in Brigham's newspaper, the *Deseret News*. Naturally, none of the editors who rewrote the stories had any clue that this was all a misunderstanding any more than the Mormons themselves did, and that President Buchanan had not, in fact, declared war on Utah.

The president knew otherwise, of course, and he was grateful when Thomas L. Kane, a longtime friend of the Mormon cause, offered to go meet with Brigham Young and explain the whole thing. The problem was that Utah was virtually snowed in by then and the mission was too urgent to be held over until spring. Kane was forced to catch a ship bound for Panama, then trek over to the Pacific side to go by ship to California and then travel overland again into Salt Lake City.

But the worst of his trip wasn't over yet. After convincing Brigham that the president had had the best of intentions, even if he wasn't very good at communicating them, Kane was given permission to personally escort the new governor into the territory after promising that no soldiers would be with them. Next he had to trudge through the snow over to Fort Bridger and convince Cumming that he could expect a friendly welcome. Kane was taken at his word, but it was quite a bit tougher to convince General Johnston that if he sent troops in that direction, all bets would be off.

When the new governor and his emissary arrived at the mouth of Echo Canyon in early April, they were met there by a company of the Nauvoo Legion in full dress uniform, sent out to be their honor guard for the rest of the journey. And the band played "Yankee Doodle." But all was not yet forgiven. When they arrived in the city itself, they found it completely deserted. Even Brigham himself had left town. The Mormons still weren't convinced that the US Army wasn't on its way, and they were preparing themselves for the worst.

When word reached Brigham that Cumming had arrived, he rode back into the city. After a series of meetings, the new governor sent a letter to General Johnston asserting that, "I have been everywhere recognized as the Governor of Utah . . . [and] have been universally greeted with such respectful attentions as are due to the representative of the executive authority of the United States in the Territory." In other words, "call off the dogs."

But Johnston still wasn't ready to do that. Part of his mission, as he saw it, was to protect federal officials in Utah, and that still remained to be done. It was, after all, United States policy to establish a military presence in every territory. But Brigham wasn't going to back off, either. His people had abandoned their homes on his orders and he doggedly refused to issue the order that would bring them back. The stalemate went on for nearly two months in the otherwise silent city.

Peace commissioners were sent out from Washington, but their diplomacy couldn't shake Brigham's resolve, nor could he get them to admit that the great United States government had made a mistake. The truth was that both sides had. The problem was that they were all too stubborn to admit it.

The standoff came to a reasonably peaceful end after Buchanan issued a presidential proclamation. Beginning by listing all of the country's grievances, real or imagined, against the Mormons, it went on to promise the Saints "full pardon and amnesty" in return for allowing troops on their soil and their promise to respect and obey the laws of the United States.

Brigham sniffed, "I thank President Buchanan for forgiving me, but I really cannot tell what I have done." In the end, he agreed to allow the military presence, but not within the confines of Salt Lake City, and the soldiers were given a campground about twenty-five

Right: *Brigham Young demonstrated remarkable resolve in the face of pressure from Washington to obey US laws. When President Buchanan offered him a "full pardon and amnesty," he quipped, "I thank President Buchanan for forgiving me, but I really cannot tell what I have done."*

miles away in a god-forsaken place called Cedar Valley. The Mormons were also given written assurance that no one would be interfered with or molested "in the peaceful pursuit of his avocation." Read: "His participation in Church rites and rituals."

Brigham waited until the troops had passed through the city on the way to their encampment and then he told his people that they could go back to their homes as soon as the camp followers had moved on as well. The sad story of misunderstanding eventually had a happy outcome, but only a Mormon might have seen the irony in it.

When the Civil War broke out three years later, the troops at Cedar Valley were ordered into combat elsewhere, and to prevent their supplies from falling into enemy hands, the government sold them to the Mormons, who had already made a handsome profit selling the army the stuff in the first place. It was like the Gold Rush all over again.

Chapter 9
A New Lease on Life

The military occupation of Utah wasn't without its problems. Church gatherings were reduced and subdued to avoid incidents that might provoke the troops, and the soldiers were occasionally deployed where they weren't welcome. But all in all, Saints and soldiers kept a wary distance from each other and most of the problems between them were minor. But, still, it was a joyful day when the army marched away. Now the Saints could get down to business again.

Work on the temple had gone forward during those years when Utah was an armed camp, but the people's mood was generally somber. When the transcontinental telegraph line reached Salt Lake City in 1861, the first message that went out over it was from Brigham Young to the new president, Abraham Lincoln. "Utah has not seceded," it said, "but is firm for the Constitution and laws of our once happy country." The reference was to the gathering war between the States, but Brigham understood that, as far as his people were concerned, happiness might be just around the corner. He knew that the war news was going to push the Mormons off the front pages, and that they would be able to get on with their lives in their own way without interference from the distracted Gentiles.

An assortment of war refugees and draft dodgers greatly increased traffic on the California-bound trails, and many Gentiles went no further than Salt Lake City. Among them were small businessmen who set up shop in competition with the Mormon entrepreneurs, but they all thrived together until the post-war depression hit and potential customers stopped passing through. It was devastating to Saints and Gentiles alike, and Brigham's response was to neutralize the competition by combining all of the various Mormon businesses in the Territory into a single enterprise he called Zion's Cooperative

Below: President Abraham Lincoln. Brigham Young telegraphed Lincoln a single line in 1861: "Utah has not seceded."

Mercantile Institution. As he already had known it would, it had the effect of eliminating the disturbing influence of the outsiders and it put the Saints a step further along the way to self-sufficiency.

Long before the war, the Stake of Zion had spread outward, and by the 1850s, less than a quarter of the Saints were living in Salt Lake City. The rest were spread out in dozens of towns along the west side of the mountains, and not all of them were populated by people who went there by choice. Brigham kept a close paternal eye on all of his people, no matter how scattered they became. When he perceived a need, a shoemaker in Bountiful, say, or experienced Welsh miners in Coalsville, he would call for volunteers and paint glowing pictures of

Below: *Lincoln's inauguration on the steps of the Capitol signaled the irrevocable slide into the Civil War. In fact, the war took the spotlight away from Mormon affairs and allowed the Saints to get on with their lives without interference.*

The Missionary Effort

Now that the Saints had established a permanent foothold in Utah, they adopted a policy of consolidating their numbers by expanding their missionary activities in Europe. Starting in England, from whence 20,000 immigrants had already come to Salt Lake City, the search for recruits was extended to France, Germany, Scandinavia (particularly Denmark) and even Palestine. Brigham Young's invention –The Perpetual Emigrating Fund– made it relatively easy for European converts to get to America. They were encouraged to bring the tools of their trades with them, which then had to be carried across the continent to their new home.

Right: *As this contemporary drawing shows, life belowdecks on immigrant ships was far from comfortable.*

Below: *A group of immigrants photographed while waiting to board their ship in Plymouth Harbour, England, to travel to New York on the first stage of their journey west to Salt Lake City.*

Above: *Brigham Young and his wife Amelia Folson. He invented the idea of the handcart trail.*

the places he was sending them to, in hopes that he wouldn't have to resort to raw authority to get them to relocate. It was a different story with the bishops, priests and others who needed to accompany them. They were simply told where they were going, and went without question. It had been the same in selecting missionaries all the way back to the days of Joseph Smith. Whenever there was a need to fill anywhere in the world, likely prospects were simply sent off, usually at a moment's notice, regardless of their family obligations or their ability to pay for the journey, which they were expected to do themselves.

The Saints became part of the American capitalist society in other ways, too. In their efforts to become self-sufficient, they were determined not to buy goods manufactured back East and shipped to them at great cost if it was at all possible to make these things for themselves. Sometimes their schemes didn't work out, like the attempt at iron mining: the ore was there, but there wasn't enough fuel or water to refine it. They had similar problems with a lead smelter, and an early dream of refining sugar failed, although it led to extensive growing of sugar beets, which became a major local industry, typical of the Mormon willingness to keep looking for new ways to cope with failure. All of these attempts to create new industries were initially financed by the Church through the proceeds of tithing. The Church accepted the losses when they came, but it also profited from the successes.

The people themselves profited individually from less ambitious projects that served the needs of their neighbors. Such things as saddleries, lumber mills and flour mills were part of every settlement and most of the small businesses prospered.

Everything the Church attempted was either to provide work for the gathered Saints or to enhance their living standards, as well as insuring its own survival. Among its grand successes was the Deseret Telegraph Company, built after the coast-to-coast wires came through; and when the transcontinental railroad was opened by joining east-west routes in Utah, Brigham saw it as an easier way for converts to get to Zion, and the Church profited from the construction of feeder lines into every corner of the Territory. Although it would be a profit-making venture, Brigham knew from bitter experience that there had to be a better way to get the Saints to the promised land.

Immigrants had been coming in waves since the very first summer, and the well-organized Mormons had made it possible with what amounted to a shuttle service of wagon trains going back and forth between the Missouri River and the valley. But during the unusually harsh winter of 1855/56, nearly all of the horses, mules, and oxen that served the enterprise starved or froze to death by the thousands in the winter pastures, and the spring migration had to be canceled.

As usual, Brigham found a solution. Noting that although wagons had accompanied them on their trek to the West, most of the previous emigrants actually walked the whole way. That being the case, he said, future emigrants could easily push small handcarts carrying their personal belongings. Work began immediately to start building them.

Each cart, divided among the Saints at a ratio of one for every five persons, carried seventeen pounds of baggage, including food, bedding, and clothing, and a fully loaded cart weighed about a hundred pounds. It ran on four-foot wooden wheels with iron tires, and each cart included a pair of five-foot-long wooden shafts that could be used to push or pull it. An ox-drawn wagon was provided for every hundred persons to carry their provisions and five tents for their camps. There was usually enough space in the wagon for the elderly to ride, but more than 3,000 reached the Salt Lake Valley on foot.

Above: *One of many evocative paintings depicting the struggle overland with handcarts.*

Below: *A preserved example of a handcart.*

The Handcart Pioneers

Between 1856 and 1860, Brigham Young initiated an experiment to encourage Mormon immigrants to walk the 1,900 miles across the plains to the West with handcarts.

The bleak winter of 1855/56 had left most of the draft animals frozen to death. Brigham Young rationalized that, as most of the immigrants walked alongside the wagons, rather than riding in them, they had actually walked to Salt Lake City. This being the case, he figured that they could walk the same journey, pushing light handcarts to carry their personal possessions. He decreed that the expeditions should be divided into companies named after their leaders.

Each cart was designed to carry seventeen pounds of baggage. Fully loaded, the carts weighed around a hundred pounds.

But the experiment nearly ended as soon as it began. The Martin company of immigrants set out with handcarts to travel across Iowa in 1856. They reached Florence, Nebraska, in August, but instead of holing up at Elkhorn for the winter, they pressed on. This was a terrible mistake. On their journey to Salt Lake City, the pioneers got caught

Above: *A contemporary illustration shows a handcart company making the fatal decision to press onwards, despite the onset of winter.*

by the full onslaught of a dreadful winter. Some of the handcarts failed due to shoddy construction, with disastrous consequences. The pioneers were forced to seek shelter in Martin's Cove, but it was too late to save the fifty-six members of the company who had already died from exposure.

Right: *The Knaphus handcart sculpture commemorates the bravery and tenacity of the handcart pioneers*

The need for such a creative solution was desperate. Four years earlier, the establishment of the Perpetual Emigrating Fund had made it relatively easy for European converts to get to America, and thousands were taking advantage of its generous terms. Even before the fund was established, more than 20,000 English immigrants—about a third of the total of new Americans from the British Isles—were already living and working in the Salt Lake Valley, and their success was an important part of the Mormon missionaries' appeal to others back in England, creating an impressive backlog of people hoping to join them.

The Emigrating Fund had made it easy for them to be able to follow. Any worthy Saint could sail to New York or New Orleans in shipboard space arranged by the Church, and the fund administrators also arranged for them to be taken by train or river steamer to camps where wagon trains were waiting to take them out across the prairie. The cost was low, but any family that couldn't afford to pay was advanced money from the fund. These people were given jobs and land in the valley, and they were expected to repay the loans with the money going directly back into the fund so that others like them could come home to Zion. Most repaid the loans as quickly as they could, but those who fell behind in their payments faced the wrath of Brigham Young—something everyone knew was best avoided, no matter what it cost.

The missionary effort had expanded beyond England into France, Germany, Italy, the Scandinavian countries, and even to Palestine. It also extended to what turned out to be rocky ground in South America, China, and India. But the

Below: An anvil brought all the way from Europe so that a blacksmith could pursue his craft in New Zion. Although these items were bulky and cumbersome to transport all the way from Europe, they were more valuable than gold in the newly established Salt Lake City.

seeds of Mormonism found fertile ground in northern Europe, and created a mini melting pot in the midst of America's own welcome to the huddled masses yearning to be free. But these immigrants were different, of course. They were all Latter-day Saints.

In those days before reception centers like Ellis Island were established, new arrivals usually found themselves at the mercy of sharpies who claimed to have the key to the Golden Door, but

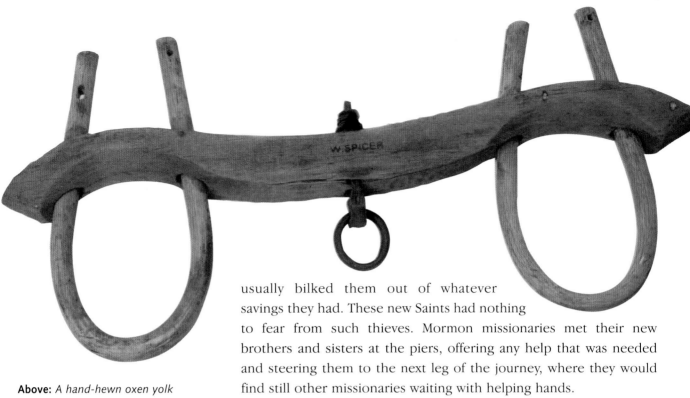

Above: *A hand-hewn oxen yolk marked with its owner's name— W. Spicer. This was an extremely useful piece of equipment.*

usually bilked them out of whatever savings they had. These new Saints had nothing to fear from such thieves. Mormon missionaries met their new brothers and sisters at the piers, offering any help that was needed and steering them to the next leg of the journey, where they would find still other missionaries waiting with helping hands.

It was never very hard to spot the Mormons in the usual immigrant mix. Many arrived on ships that had been exclusively chartered for them, but those who didn't were separated into their own sections of the steerage quarters of regular ships. They invariably organized themselves into wards under the care of missionaries who led them in prayer and hymn-signing. Most ship captains were pleased to have passengers who policed themselves, but few were happy with the baggage that had to be stowed for them. Most immigrants traveled light, sometimes with a whole family's belongings in a single bag, but the Mormon converts had been told to take along tools of their trades, which would be valuable to the Saints in Zion, and their luggage was sometimes weighted down with such things as carpentry tools, sewing machines, and light farm equipment.

The first waves of the fund-financed immigrants arrived in America at New Orleans and then went by boat up the Mississippi to St. Louis for a transfer to another boat that would take them 500 miles up the Missouri River to the jumping-off place at the edge of the Great Plains. New York, Boston, and Philadelphia became the main debarkation ports after the railroad reached St. Louis, and the journey became a bit easier. But it still took nine months or more for a family to make its way from its old home to the new one.

Brigham Young's handcart scheme was financed by the Perpetual Emigrating Fund, with the substantial cost savings passed along to the immigrants. For the first time, its benefits were extended to new converts from the Eastern states as well. The plan dramatically lowered their cost of going west, and thousands responded as soon as it was announced; although, predictably, not all of them were so sure that they liked the idea of walking halfway across the country.

Above: *A dramatic oil painting depicting the terrible plight of the Martin handcart company, many of whom perished in the harsh winter of 1856.*

The first of the handcart companies stepped out from Iowa City in early June 1856. There were 1,900 of them, mostly new arrivals from England and Wales, divided into five companies, each leaving at scheduled intervals. The first wave reached the Missouri River three weeks later, averaging about twenty miles a day, but they were determined to step up the pace once their legs stopped hurting.

The food in the supply wagons was doled out every second day at

the rate of a pound of flour and smaller portions of tea, coffee, sugar, and rice for each individual. Cows tagging along behind gave them fresh milk, and a herd of beef cattle provided them with meat, as long as they were careful not to slaughter them too quickly. A few of the companies were also lucky enough to kill a buffalo or two along the way.

The first two handcart companies arrived in the Salt Lake Valley at the end of September after having walked 1,900 miles in nine weeks, and no company of Saints had ever been given a warmer welcome. Brigham Young himself led a delegation of Mormon VIPs out to greet them. The Nauvoo Legion and the brass band went along with them, and the last couple of miles of their trek turned into a parade through Salt Lake City with cheering Saints lining the streets.

There were Gentiles living in their midst by then, and it had become critical to increase the population of Saints as a counterbalance. Once again, Brigham Young had shown them the way to do it, but they would soon find out that handcarts weren't the perfect answer. The last two companies out of the Iowa City railhead wouldn't be nearly as lucky as the first.

Extra handcarts needed to be built to handle these late arrivals, and in the rush to get them finished, the missionaries were forced to buy green lumber, even if it was against their better judgment. It made the carts a good bit heavier, and because they were forced to leave with fewer than the standard number of supply wagons, each handcart carried about a hundred pounds of flour and other food. But that was only the first problem.

This last wave of about 900 Saints started across the plains in early August and the hot sun caused the green wood to start shrinking. It meant that they had to stop frequently for repairs, especially to the wheels when the iron rims fell off because of the shrinkage, which also caused the wooden axles to fall loose. The result was that it took them more than twice as long to reach the Missouri as the companies that had gone before them.

But even though they were beginning to fall short of food by then, their spirits were still relatively high and they pressed on. What they didn't know was that the winter storms would start raging quite a bit earlier than usual that year, and that they'd be tramping through snow by early October.

It was snowing in the valley too, and Brigham knew that the last wave would never make it unless he organized a rescue mission right away. As a hundred horse-and-mule teams set out to face the dangers of the snowy mountains, he made a vow never to allow companies to cross the prairie this late in the season again. "It is a great mistake," he said ruefully. It wasn't until after the wandering Saints were rescued that anyone realized what a huge mistake it had been.

It was a rare wagon train that didn't experience hardship and

Below and bottom of page: *The Mormon pioneers established way stations, such as Cove Fort, along the migration routes to provide shelter for travelers.*

death on the journeys that opened the American West, but these two companies of handcart emigrants easily experienced the worst conditions that God and nature could throw in their path. Few westward-bound companies, Mormon or Gentile, had a more horrifying story to tell.

There was no hint of the ordeal ahead when they started out. They averaged about fifteen miles a day during the first week, and on good days, they covered twenty. Even after their carts started breaking down, they rarely made fewer than ten miles a day. They began encountering buffalo herds after they reached the Wood River about halfway across Nebraska, and one of the herds was spotted running at full speed directly into the path of one of the companies, a terrifying sight to people on foot in open country. For some reason, the huge animals abruptly turned before they reached the line of people, but the thundering noise they were making made the train's livestock stampede. After three days of searching for their lost animals, the Saints came to the realization that thirty of them were lost and gone forever, and there was nothing they could do but press their beef cattle and milk cows into service to pull the supply wagons. Some of the food was packed into their handcarts to lighten the animals' burden and they trudged on.

Below: *A spectacular painting shows Chimney Rock, one of the fantastic sites along the trail.*

When a cart broke down, the column kept moving on and the owner stayed behind to repair it as best he could. But sometimes these men fell so far behind that they simply abandoned their carts and the supplies they contained and walked on to make sure they'd reach the safety of the camp before the sun went down.

It was in one of those camps that they met a company of Apostles and missionaries on its way back from a mission to the East. The visitors were reassured that God would get them to Zion safely, as long as they remained "faithful, prayerful and obedient." The missionaries gave them some practical advice–traveling would be easier on the south side of the Platte River–and after guiding the visitors there, they moved on with a promise to send a relief company out to meet them.

The Saints hoped that they would be able to get resupplied at Laramie, which wasn't much further along, but when they got there, there was nothing to spare. They had determined that the food they were carrying would run out a few hundred miles shy of their destination, and the already meager ration was cut in half. It had to be cut once again by the time they reached Independence Rock. Men who pulled carts were reduced to twelve ounces of food a day; the elderly–and there were many of them–were forced to survive on nine ounces, and children on four. At the same time, they were ordered to start walking a little faster.

Above: *Converts arriving in the United States were greeted by brothers and sisters from the Church in an attempt to protect them from the many tricksters preying on new arrivals.*

Winter had firmly set in by the time the Saints reached the Sweetwater River, and they had no warm clothing. They had very little energy left, and their companions were dying by the dozens from dysentery and exhaustion. The last company alone lost sixty-seven of its 400 members. The tragedy compounded itself by leaving many women widows and many children orphans. The survivors were forced to double

their efforts to take care of them. Meanwhile, snow piled up in the path of their carts and wagons, and their already slow march turned to a crawl. They had reached a point about fifty miles southwest of present-day Casper, Wyoming.

The missionaries came back again with word that the rescue party was right behind them and that gave the emigrants fresh hope. But later

105

that same afternoon a blizzard came instead, dumping twelve inches of new snow in their path. They voted not to try pushing through it, and agreed to stay where they were until the promised help arrived.

But that same storm had also stalled the relief train, and it didn't arrive until after three long days and nights had passed. Several more of the handcart emigrants had died in the camp by then, and the rest were all about ready to give up. But the sight of friendly faces and the food and warm clothing they brought changed everything in the twinkling of an eye. The evening was filled with the singing of hymns, prayer, and, for the first time in weeks, laughter.

The Salt Lake Mormons accepted the handcart tragedy as another sign from God that they weren't worthy to inherit God's Kingdom unless they changed their ways. Their detractors in the outside world took it as another sign of what they regarded as the Saints' intrinsic evilness, adding greed and disregard for human life to their bill of particulars.

In spite of the tragedy, the pipeline between England and America was overflowing with hopeful converts, and the handcart trek had to be continued over the following three seasons, but the concept was quietly dropped in 1860.

Immigration into the territory almost never stopped and the Saints prospered in their promised land with the help of the new arrivals, but the wolves of anti-Mormonism were never very far away—and they appeared to be closing in.

A federal law prohibiting polygamy went on the books in 1862, and after about ten years of waiting for the government to drop the other shoe, Brigham Young was finally arrested on charges of violating it. He was acquitted in the show trial that followed, but the government didn't stop there. The federal authorities attempted to prove his complicity in the Mountain Meadow massacre in 1877, twenty years after the incident, by bringing John Lee to trial for his admitted part in it. They weren't able to prove their suspicions about the Mormon leader's involvement, but when Lee was acquitted, a second trial was ordered on a charge that Brigham had unduly influenced the all-Mormon jury. The second jury sentenced Lee to death, and Brigham accepted their verdict for the good of the Church.

Brigham Young died a few weeks after the second trial, leaving his people to face no end of trials of their own as the federal government tried everything in its power to strip them of the political and economic influence they had built up while Brigham still lived.

A few years before Brigham died, Ulysses S. Grant became the country's president and he let it be known to one and all that he was dedicating himself to wiping out what he called "licensed prostitution" in the Utah Territory. He was referring to polygamy, of course, an issue that had raised its ugly head again through the efforts of former abolitionists who were looking for a new cause, and was now garnering even more momentum from a new breed of women's rights activists. Grant's first order was to abolish the Nauvoo Legion, which still existed as the local militia. Although every state had similar local armed protective forces, territories did not, and Grant leveled the playing field as a first step toward planting federal authority in Utah.

Grant's next step was to reform the courts, and James B. McKean, his appointed territorial chief justice, announced that his court was not subject to local law, and that he was disregarding the authority of the marshal, who controlled the jury pool, and the attorney general who served as the territory's prosecutor. The Mormon-run legislature responded by withdrawing funds from what they were being told had become federal and not territorial courts, and the judge was forced to dismiss jurors because he didn't have the money to pay them.

But McKean said that he had no intention of leaving, even if his hands had been tied. "The day is not too far off in the future when the high priesthood of the so-called Church of Jesus Christ of Latter-day Saints shall bow to and obey the laws that are elsewhere respected, or those laws will grind them to powder," he announced. The gauntlet had been thrown down.

Fortunately for the Church, and the Saints who relied on its strength, it had highly motivated leaders who were able and more than willing to take up the challenge. Brigham's successor was John Taylor, the former President of the Quorum of the Twelve Apostles. This was the same John Taylor who had been imprisoned with Joseph Smith on that fateful night back at the Carthage Jailhouse.

There didn't seem to be much that was bothering the Gentiles by 1877, except for that overwhelming issue of polygamy. The law already on the books prohibiting plural marriage was riddled with loopholes, and both sides had come to a standoff over enforcing it. At the time, Congress was debating another bill designed to put teeth into the law by defining polygamy as "unlawful cohabitation" and setting punishment for the crime at denial of the right to vote, the right to hold public office, or the right to serve on juries in cases involving such unions.

The Mormons themselves had become resigned to the fact that the bill would eventually become law, although they knew very well that it was aimed squarely at Church leaders who were facing the prospect of being convicted of a newly crafted federal offense without the right of a trial. They also objected to the use of the term "unlawful cohabitation," which by inference extended to pimps and prostitutes, not to mention garden-variety adulterers. But they knew that the battle had been lost, and they faced up to it. As one of the Elders put it, "If the nation can stand it, so can we."

The bill passed and was signed into law in 1882, after which John Taylor sent five of his six wives back to their own families in order to avoid the indignity of being arrested and tried. He made it clear that he considered the law discriminatory, even if he appeared to be agreeing to abide by it. "We will fulfill the letter, so far as is practical, of that unjust, inhuman, oppressive, and unconstitutional law, so far as we can without violating principle," he said.

But if President Taylor managed to escape prosecution, others did not. The first to appear in court on charges of polygamy were two women, one of whom was released because of the imminent birth of her child. The other stared down her accusers and said that she had been planning to divorce her husband anyway, but she still defended her marriage as being "of God" and told the court that it was none of its business in the first place.

A young Mormon hero named Rudgar Clawson was the most celebrated of hundreds of such defendants. When he appeared before the judge, he said, "I very much regret that if the laws of my country should come in conflict with the laws of God, I shall inevitably choose the latter." He was convicted anyway for the crime of having two wives, and he was fined $800 and sentenced to four years in jail. Clawson had an otherwise spotless reputation, and President Taylor noted in a statement that he would be a free man if he had done what "tens of thousands of others do, live in conditions of illicit love. And then if any child should result from this unsanctified union, why not follow our Christian exemplars, remove the fetal encumbrance, call in some . . . abortionist, male or female, that pollute our land? That would have been . . . genteel, fashionable, respectable, Christian-like, as Christianity goes in this generation."

But Washington wasn't finished with the Mormons yet. The antipolygamy law had been touted as a means of protecting all American families, but only Mormon families were actually affected by it. The legalized discrimination would get worse four years later when yet another law emerged, officially called the Edmunds-Tucker Act, but more often called the "Utah Act." Among other things, it voided Utah's women's suffrage law, the first and only one in the nation. It dissolved the Church as a corporate entity, confiscated its funds, and put strict limits on how they could be rebuilt. Under its terms, spouses could be forced to testify against one another, and charges of sexual offenses could be brought by persons with no firsthand knowledge of the alleged acts. Although this was a federal law, its provisions applied only in territories, and not in states, in spite of the fact that all American citizens were protected by the same Constitution no matter where they happened to live.

Among other indignities visited upon the Saints, when Elder George Q. Cannon was reelected to his fifth term as territorial delegate to Congress in 1880, a federal judge voided the election on the grounds that he was a Mormon and therefore not an American citizen, which made him ineligible to go back to Washington. Nearly all of his constituents were Mormons, of course, so he went anyway and he was seated. But after a series of hearings two years later, Elder

Cannon's seat was taken away from him and it remained vacant until the next election.

The decade of the 1880s was not a happy time in Zion. It wasn't uncommon for federal officers to break into homes in the dead of night looking for evidence of "cohabitation," which a court had ruled didn't necessarily have to involve sexual relations, and tracking down possible offenders wherever their spies told the sex police they might be found. Many homeowners added escape doors to their houses to allow the men to make fast getaways when danger was threatening, and some built secret rooms where they could hide out until the danger had passed. Every stranger who passed through was both suspected and feared, and with good reason. Any male in the territory could be arrested on the spot without specific charges, and the jails were filled with men who refused to denounce their Church, leaving their wives and children behind to fend for themselves. Although the "cohabs," as the prisoners were called, were allowed to hold religious services in the jails, this was not what they had expected in the Land of the Free. This was America, where such things weren't supposed to happen.

The prime targets of the harassing federal agents were the Church's leaders, and Church meetings were usually held on short notice at remote locations, although most of the leadership was either in hiding or in jail and the meetings were short and poorly attended. Even President Taylor felt that it was best if he himself went into hiding, and he died in his self-imposed exile at Kaysville.

Taylor and his followers had always had complete faith that the United States Supreme Court would find the Utah Act unconstitutional, but that faith had been misplaced. The court ultimately upheld the law, and the lawmakers in Washington readied to bring more legislative grief down upon the Saints and their Church.

Their efforts became moot when the new Church President, Wilford Woodruff, issued what was called the "Manifesto" in September 1890. Although it officially ended polygamy as a Church doctrine once and for all, President Woodruff made it a point not to denounce the practice itself. He simply stated that because it had become contrary to the law of the land, "I hereby declare my intention to submit to those laws, and to use my influence with the members of the Church over which I preside to have them do likewise."

The new President pointed out that the Church of Jesus Christ of Latter-day Saints honored a great many religious principles that were infinitely more important to them than plural marriage, which he characterized as "an onerous burden of God's law that is too heavy to be carried by mankind in its present state of imperfection."

Chief among the principles Woodruff championed was the belief that a new kingdom of God had been established through Joseph

Smith in preparation for Christ's Second Coming in the latter days. President Woodruff recalled that Joseph had attempted to create a political entity, as well as a kingdom of faith, but although its political aspects had been left in shambles, it was the urgent duty of every Saint to preserve the spiritual kingdom from threatened destruction as well. He reminded his people that the new Millennium was imminent, and it was going to involve the establishment of a worldwide Church with Jesus Christ Himself at its head. The political side of their movement was going to be replaced by the Millennial Church anyway, and it was undoubtedly going to happen sooner rather than later. All the Saints needed to do was wait patiently.

Clearly the Saints had entered a new era, but the issue of polygamy was still in their midst. Although the practice had technically been outlawed by both church and state, the status of families already sealed in plural marriages was still up in the air. What followed next wasn't regarded as a miracle, but it might have been. Nearly all of the federal judges in the territory suddenly, and independently, had an abrupt change of heart. Generally, when a defendant in a polygamy action was asked if he agreed with the Manifesto, the case was dismissed if he swore that he did. Three years after the law went into effect, President Benjamin Harrison issued a general amnesty to any Saints who had complied with the law since the issuance of the Manifesto, which emptied the jails, and the forgiveness was soon extended to benefit the entire Mormon community.

The only remaining step to acceptance of the Saints as full-fledged American citizens was to dissolve their local political parties in favor of participation in the national organizations. Most became Democrats in the belief that Republican politicians had been the source of most of their past grief, which certainly did appear to be the case. And in the interest of keeping their political fences in good repair, the leadership goaded many into registering as Republicans and letting the dead past be buried. But as it turned out, it was Republicans in Congress who pushed hardest for statehood and it was largely due to their influence that Utah finally became the forty-fifth state in the Union on January 4, 1896.

The Saints had come a long way, but the struggles of their last two decades on the outside looking in had taken a terrible toll. Typically, though, they weren't given to licking their wounds, and they were already hard at work picking up the pieces.

Chapter 10
Tradition

I n the Old Testament Book of Leviticus, the Lord tells his people, "And ye shall hallow the fiftieth year and proclaim liberty throughout all of the land unto all the inhabitants thereof: It shall be a jubilee unto you; and ye shall return every man unto his possession, and ye shall return every man unto his family."

For the Latter-day Saints, the Year of Jubilee was 1880, the fiftieth anniversary of the founding of their Church. Following the lead of the ancient Israelites, the Church officially wiped out the debts of the "worthy poor" among its members, many of whom still owed money to the Perpetual Emigration Fund, and those among the poor who were behind in their tithing payments found that obligation cut in half. A severe drought the previous year had cut crop yields dramatically and the silos of the Relief Society were opened to suffering farmers who were loaned grain until they could get back on their feet again. President Taylor also encouraged, although he didn't order, the more affluent Saints to forgive all debts "to free the worthy debt-bound brother."

The Church itself was thriving at the time of the Jubilee Year. It was a time for expanding Zion, and Mormon settlements had been

Above: *Brigham Young University, Hawaii.*

Left: *A beautiful and ornate baptismal font in the Temple at Accra, Ghana.*

springing up as far afield as Arizona and Nevada, Colorado and Wyoming. As their persecutors bore down on them, many Mormons had moved on to the relative safety of Mexico, although it took some doing to be able to buy land there, or even to settle on leased property. Yet they persevered, and by the late 1880s, some 3,000 Saints had resettled in three colonies south of the border. Others pushed on to Canada and soon had a large enough population there to establish its own stake in the province of Alberta.

But although the Mormons were master colonizers, they were even better missionaries, and the proselytizing had not let up for a moment since Joseph Smith's brother Samuel had gone out into the countryside and harvested Brigham Young.

In the early 1880s, a successful Mormon branch was established in New Zealand, where a Maori chief was ordained to the priesthood and led his people into the Church. There was a similar growth of membership among the Polynesians in Hawaii. A Mormon mission in Turkey opened the Church to German expatriates living in the original land of Zion, and the always-thriving European missions were expanding as fast as was humanly possible. In some places, England and the Scandinavian countries, for instance, local officials gingerly suggested that the Mormon out-migration should stop or at least slow down, not because they were worried about losing their brightest and

Above: *A view of downtown Salt Lake City showing Church Plaza with its curious mix of traditional and modern architecture. The greenery of the site is evident—a true oasis in the desert.*

best to America, but because of the colored news reports coming out of Utah and strong pressure from the American government itself to slow the growth of the Mormon Church. President Grover Cleveland even went so far as to propose a law making foreign immigration into Utah illegal. But the Church kept growing in spite of all these attempts to curb its influence.

The 1862 law not only dissolved the Church as a political entity, but limited its assets to $50,000. That rule was all but unenforceable, but a new law, passed twenty years later, called for transferring Church

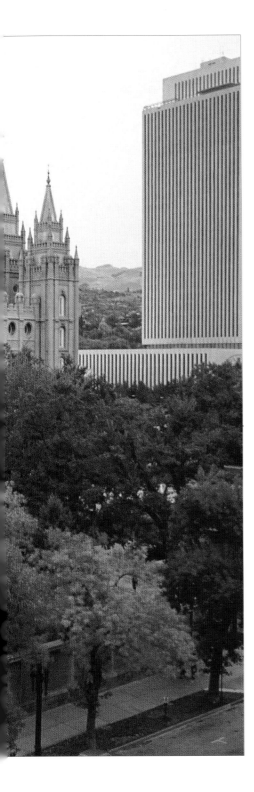

property over to the government, which would appoint a receiver to administer it. But even before the law went into effect, affluent private citizens were asked to take over some of the properties in question as part of their private portfolios to be held in trust for the Church. Other properties, such as temples, were signed over to nonprofit organizations, and new associations, set up as private enterprises, took title to the Bishop's warehouses and their contents being held in reserve for the needy, as well as most of the meetinghouses and tithing houses.

Naturally, the federal authorities saw this for what it was. The appointed receiver, the local US marshal, immediately seized all of the property the Church hadn't disposed of by then and leased it back to them on his terms. Then he went after the associations and private individuals who were in control of the rest. Arguing that all of this was actually Church property hiding behind false whiskers, he relieved them collectively of nearly $1 million in property and assets. In spite of their confidence that the Supreme Court would uphold their claim that this was an unconstitutional violation of their property rights and their right to enter into contracts, the Court ultimately ruled otherwise. The Saints were left without a way to fund their day-to-day Church operations, not to mention such things as missionary work and temple building.

In many ways the financial crisis was as important to the evolution of the newly shaped Church of Jesus Christ of Latter-day Saints as the Manifesto had been in doing away with its intention of becoming an earthly political kingdom. Without that goal, their need for funds had lessened considerably, and the source of money to build and maintain a spiritual kingdom had been with them all along.

President Lorenzo Snow reminded them of that after receiving a revelation that he said called on him and all of the Saints to fall back on "the Lord's law of revenue." It was tithing he had in mind, and he made the rounds of all of the congregations in Utah to spread the message that the Saints had been neglecting the law of tithing, but that the Lord had revealed to him that if every Saint faithfully paid a full tithe, "blessings would be showered upon them." The record seems to indicate that he was right. Within less than seven years, largely thanks to faithful tithing, the Church had paid off all of its creditors and was completely debt-free for the first time since their troubles began.

Of course, there was more to it than that. President Snow had evolved into a kind of financial genius. As the Church marched into the twentieth century, he decreed that it should stop borrowing for investment, sell its interest in most of the businesses it had helped establish, and borrow money for its own operation and expansion "among ourselves, rather than go into the world." He also instituted a million-dollar bond issue to retire some of the Church's debt, carefully making it available only within the Church family. The first half was paid off in the first four years and the rest in three more. He also strongly urged the Saints to avoid personal indebtedness, and most of them were as proud of themselves as of their Church when President Joseph F. Smith announced in 1907, "The Church of Jesus Christ of Latter-day Saints owes not a dollar that it cannot pay at once. At last we are in a position that we can pay as we go."

Little by little in the prosperity of the pre–World War I years, the Church quietly began moving back into the world of business. One of the first steps was the formation of the Utah-Idaho Sugar Company, a merger of several smaller operations that made it more profitable for Mormon farmers to grow sugar beets. It was a significant break from the tradition of cooperative self-sufficiency with the infusion of Gentile capital, in this case from the American Sugar Refining Company. The Church itself was a minority stockholder, but the company was controlled by, and thrived under, the influence of Church leaders. Six years later, when the government dissolved American Sugar's monopoly, the Church was there to pick up its share of the pieces and acquired full control of the local subsidiary for itself.

The Church had been less covert in its ownership of the elegant Hotel Utah near Temple Square in Salt Lake City, an enterprise that the leadership had promoted as a way of keeping the downtown neighborhood vital. They came in for strong criticism, though, when

Below: *The Family History Library in Salt Lake City.*

Above: *The stunning San Diego Temple at night.*

Below: *The Museum of Church History and Art in Salt Lake City.*

the hotel's operating company opened a bar, which was against Mormon principles and added insult to injury because of its nearness to the Temple. President Smith defused the critics by pointing out that the Saints in Salt Lake City had already overwhelmingly voted down a referendum on local prohibition of alcohol, and visitors to the city, which wasn't otherwise dry, expected "something to wet up with" when they came to town. The bar stayed open, and the Utah became the hotel of choice for thirsty visitors. Significantly, although the Church was foursquare on the side of the later Prohibition amendment to the Constitution, Utah cast the deciding vote to ratify the amendment that repealed it in 1933. In typical Mormon fashion, the Church turned the negative into a positive with a statement that it was proof once and for all that the Church of Jesus Christ of Latter-day Saints had no control over politics in Utah.

The new philosophy that emerged in the early twentieth century was that conservative investment by the Church would not only boost its income directly, but would benefit its members, who would then pay more in tithing. With that in mind, they acquired the profitable Provo Woolen Mills and controlled a host of small businesses from banks to bookstores and newspapers all over the state.

The Church was a prime mover in bringing Utah in general and Salt Lake City in particular, into the American mainstream in the early

years of the twentieth century, but the ghost of the nineteenth was still haunting them. After his election to Congress in 1898, it was revealed that Elder B. H. Roberts still had several wives, whom he married before the Manifesto came into effect. Although he had benefited from the federal amnesty, he still had multiple wives, and that brought back the old animosities. It became a national scandal and dozens of petitions were circulated calling for his seat to be denied him. One of them garnered seven million signatures. A House committee debated the issue, and after six weeks of discussion, the conferees voted to send Elder Roberts back home to Utah.

In another four years, Elder Reed Smoot was elected to the United States Senate, and although he had only one wife, he also ran into a firestorm when he reached Washington. He was allowed to take his seat, but only pending a special investigation into the propriety of having a member of the Church's Council of Twelve serve in such an exalted federal position, which had all the earmarks of commingling the authority of church and state. The hearings lasted thirty months and produced more than 3,000 pages of testimony, but in the end Senator Smoot was accepted as a US Senator and he held the job for the next thirty years.

In his early years in Washington, Senator Smoot was a lightning rod for anti-Mormon muckrakers who extended their attacks on him to the Church itself. More often than not, they were rehashes of all the old arguments, true or not. Even though the Church had already put aside its goal of creating a political kingdom within the United States, the new attackers accused it of scheming to take over the federal government and then subvert traditional American family values. It would be gratifying to report that nobody paid much attention to what they were reading in magazines and newspapers about this new perceived Mormon menace, but that was not at all the case.

The negative images spread to the British press and extended into a rash of novels, often lurid tales of plural marriage and the seduction of the innocent by rapacious Mormon missionaries. Their influence resulted in violence at anti-Mormon rallies and vandalism at some of the Church's chapels. In the first decade of the twentieth century, the rate of baptisms more than doubled, but in the second, it plummeted by more than a third. As a corollary to the trend, the German government expelled the Mormon missionaries, and other European countries were debating similar actions.

The Church responded with a media blitz of its own and arranged to send the Tabernacle Choir on it first national tour, which included serenading President William Howard Taft in the East Room at the White House. They also published testimonials from popular public

Left: *The splendid facade of the Salt Lake City Conference Center at night.*

figures like former president Theodore Roosevelt, who told the American public in his own enthusiastic way how impressed he was by the Mormons' high moral standards and how pleased he was as a family man by the cohesiveness of their families.

After the end of the First World War in 1918, all of the Church's troubles seemed to be behind it. It was far from the brink of bankruptcy, and Americans had finally gotten it through their heads that polygamy was a dead issue. Leaders on speaking tours found themselves no longer on the defensive, but rather, accepting accolades from other members of the religious community. Still, there were some in that community who believed that the Church of the Latter-day Saints was itself experiencing its last days. As one Protestant leader put it, "The way to oppose Mormonism is not to throw mud upon it. A campaign of detraction only helps it to grow. The thing to do is treat it with fairness and candor . . . It must fall of its own weight if it is to fall." Of course, the Church had no intention of falling.

Above: *Eagle Gate in Salt Lake City.*

The greatest threat, as many saw it, was the same one that Brigham Young had perceived. Their trials seem to have ended, and the Saints were being endangered by their own complacency.

But the real danger was not from within. The original intent of the Mormon exodus had been to gather the Saints in one central place, call it Deseret or call it Utah. But over the years after the Civil War, nearly the entire American population was on the move, leaving farms for better jobs and a better life in the cities. The Mormons in Utah and the other mountain states were largely dependent on a rural economy, which by the 1920s, had begun to turn sour. Many Mormon families responded by picking up stakes and going job-hunting in urban areas, particularly along the West Coast. In the 1920s, the Mormon population in their traditional home base of Utah dropped by almost 5 percent, a trickle to be sure, but the handwriting was on the wall.

Opportunities in Mormon country had become quite limited, and the Church responded by discouraging any more foreign immigration. Its leaders believed that the time had come for the Saints to build the Kingdom in their own homelands, and promised them that the time was near when Temples would be established all over the world.

They also suggested that converts in America should stay where they were, and by the end of the decade stakes were created in Los

Opposite page, right: *President Gordon B. Hinckley, the fifteenth President of the Mormon Church, appointed March 12, 1995. Hinckley's grandfather was Ira Hinckley, a Mormon convert of 1844, who crossed the plains and supervised the construction of Cove Fort.*

Above: *An aerial view of the Brigham Young University campus in Utah.*

Angeles, Hollywood, and San Francisco. In 1934, another was established in New York State, effectively returning the Church to its original roots four years after the centennial of its founding.

In the early days, Joseph Smith had received a revelation on health practices, and among other things, he advised his followers to avoid coffee, tea, alcoholic beverages, and tobacco. The rules were disregarded more often than not, and in the early days of the Zion stake, travelers usually remembered the Saints' own home-distilled whiskey, called "valley tan," more than almost anything else. But in the 1930s, President Heber J. Grant promulgated the "Words of Wisdom," which made it the Church's firm policy to deny advancement in the

Above: *The Salt Lake City Tabernacle garlanded in flowers.*

Below: *The Temple in Hong Kong shows the global penetration that the Church has achieved.*

priesthood and entrance to the temples for any but total abstainers.

In the 1960s, when many young people were smoking things other than tobacco and generally dropping out of society, more of them than ever before were converting to the Mormon Church. The increase was an astounding 145 percent. The gain was even more impressive in Great Britain, where it reached 527 percent. The trend hasn't stopped yet, and the Church of Jesus Christ of Latter-day Saints is still growing at a rate of more than 30 percent a year.

Nearly all of the world's religions regard education as the cornerstone of their existence, and the Church of Latter-day Saints takes its responsibility seriously. Education has been at the heart of Mormonism since the time of Joseph Smith, and it flourished in nineteenth-century Utah when public education was a Church responsibility. The concept is flourishing still in the twenty-first century through the Church Educational System, which provides curricula and teaching staffs for Church seminaries and institutes of religion in 135 countries. The seminaries, serving secondary students, have an enrollment of more than 371,000, and the institutes of religion serve more than 356,000. The programs are administered through Brigham Young University in Provo, Utah, a Church-operated institution with a full-time day enrollment of more than 28,000 students. BYU at Rexburg, Idaho, has more than 10,000 students, and another branch of the university at Laie, Hawaii, has about 2,500 students. The Church also operates the LDS Business College at Salt Lake City with an enrollment of about 1,000, as well as nineteen elementary and secondary schools in Mexico and the Pacific islands.

Seminary students meet every day, either before school or in "released time" class periods during the school day. They meet in local Church meetinghouses or private homes and are taught by volunteers.

Left: *The Church Office Building.*
Opposite page: *The granite vault at Little Cottonwood Canyon, Utah, where important Church archives and family histories are deposited.*

In many cases, they are served by Church-owned seminary buildings, which are also open for study and for social interaction. The Institutes of Religion, serving students ages eighteen to thirty, meet in Church-owned seminary buildings or in Church meetinghouses, and the facilities are available on most college and university campuses in the United States and around the world.

Most of the teaching in underdeveloped countries is done by missionaries who until recently came home to a life of relative poverty with no funds to pay for their own education. That problem was corrected in 2001 with the establishment of the worldwide Perpetual Education Fund. Modeled after the Perpetual Emigrating Fund that made emigration possible for thousands in the nineteenth century, it provides low-interest loans from funds donated by Church members that can be repaid once the recipient has pursued an education and found a job. In announcing the program, LDS President Gordon B. Hinckley said, "Where there is widespread poverty among our people, we must do all we can to help them lift themselves, to establish their lives upon a foundation of self-reliance that can come of training. Education is the key to opportunity. This training must be done in the areas where they live. It will then be suited to the opportunities of those areas."

Although it is still considered an American church, there are more Mormon stakes outside North America than within it today. From the first temple at Kirtland, the number has passed the one-hundred mark with half again as many in some stage of construction around the world. In an interview during the 1990s, Hinckley told a reporter that "the most serious challenge we face, and the most wonderful challenge, is the challenge that comes from growth." When he assumed the presidency, he told another interviewer that his focus would be to "carry on. Yes, our theme will be to carry on the great work which has been furthered by our predecessors who have served admirably, so faithfully, and so well."

He might have added, in all honesty, "All is well!"

Index

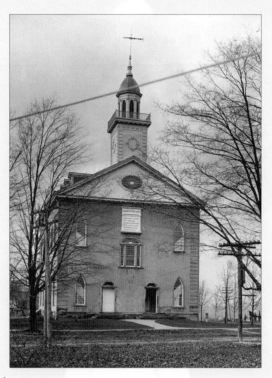

Acknowledgments

Ronald Read and Millie
Museum of Church History and Art, Salt Lake City,
for the excellent color images used in the book.
Rachel Hoover
Brigham Young University,
for the use of paintings from their collection.
Crossing the Mississippi on the ice
Exterior of Carthage Jail The Nauvoo Temple
The Battle of Nauvoo Winter Quarters
and Entering the Great Salt Lake Valley
By C.C.A. Christiansen.
All Rights reserved.

Bill Slaughter,
LDS Church Archives, Salt Lake City,
for access to the original archive photography.

John Drayton, Director, University of Oklahoma
Press,
for reading the manuscript.

Wm. Budge Wallis
for his help and support.